NOTICE ME!

A Barnardo Child's Scrapbook of
Memories:
1946 to 1961

Published by

MELROSE BOOKS

An Imprint of Melrose Press Limited
St Thomas Place, Ely
Cambridgeshire
CB7 4GG, UK
www.melrosebooks.co.uk

FIRST EDITION

Copyright © Suzi Hamilton 2012

The Author asserts her moral right to
be identified as the author of this work

Cover designed by Gwyn Law

ISBN 978-1-907732-81-2

Printed and bound in Great Britain by:
TJ International Ltd, Padstow, Cornwall

MIX
Paper from
responsible sources
FSC
www.fsc.org   FSC® C013056

FOR

Ann Forster

Dedicated to the memory of Dr Thomas John Barnardo
(1845–1905)
"The Father of Nobody's Children"

This book is based on true events, therefore all names have been changed to protect the privacy of individuals

CONTENTS

INTRODUCTION

Never in my wildest dreams did I imagine that the star of my athletics team (TVH 1958) would, in fifty years' time, ask me to edit and write an introduction to the story of her life in the 'Village'. I consider it a great privilege that Suzan has chosen me.

As this story takes place almost entirely in the Village, perhaps it would be appropriate to explain the history of the Village 'home'.

Many people have heard of Dr Barnardo and know that his work continues to this day. Not so many will know the 'Girls' Village Home' built by him at Barkingside in Ilford, Essex. After his marriage to Syrie, the couple made their home in a large house in Barkingside, and from there the doctor supervised the building of a self-contained village of sixty-four 'cottages', a school, hospital and church, to accommodate fifteen hundred girls.

From unbaptised 'coloured' baby to a 65-year-old lady today, Suzan has been seeking her own identity. This story wanders through her experiences in the Village, her schools outside the Village, and her placement on leaving school and venturing into the wider world. It also deals with her reaction to rejection, ridicule and continuous experience of colour prejudice, and despicable bullying from people into whose care she was placed and who showed nothing of the loving care and support she needed to help her through her formative years.

Suzan's story comes from the heart; she does not pull her punches. It is a very brave attempt to describe the punitive regime that was her lot for so many years, mainly because her skin was not completely white.

The reader may need a strong drink and a large box of tissues.

Dennis Vine

FOREWORD

In 1995, Dr Barnardo's 'opened their files' and, to quote a friend of mine at the time, "All hell broke loose!" The head office was inundated with requests from 'old boys' and girls to be given access to their records. At last, we hoped, we could discover who we *really* were. Had anyone cared enough about us to make enquiries, only to come up against the proverbial brick wall of silence? How would our lives be changed, if at all?

It was a frantic and distressing period, not only for the 'children', but also the office staff, as they often had to inform enquirers that family members had died or did not want to recognise them or, in many cases, had no idea they existed.

In early post-war Britain, there was a great deal of social and domestic upheaval as 'normal' families tried to re-establish themselves.

And what of the hundreds of children left in Dr Barnardo's Homes? How did *they* cope with all this? A few were eventually reunited with their families, but most remained in care, particularly the illegitimate babies born to English women and black American servicemen.

I was one of those children: a 'bulge baby', born in April 1945.

This, then, is *my* story.

I have called it a 'scrapbook' because, having only comparatively recently gained access to my records, I am still trying to piece together the fragmented picture of my true identity. Coming to terms with the resultant confusion, both emotional and spiritual, as I recall past events, is also proving a daunting process.

All the chapters, save one, are subtitled with a line or two from favourite hymns of mine. Dr Barnardo's was, and still is, a Christian charity and I think it is important to make this fact clear. The children's church in the 'Village' was very much part of my everyday life.

With regard to the use of the description 'coloured' throughout my story, I should mention that I am writing about events that occurred between 1946 and 1961, when the word 'black' was only ever used in a derogatory fashion. I therefore feel it is necessary to adhere to the original, and contemporaneous, description, in order to avoid confusion.

From a personal point of view, I wish to state as follows:

My 'pedigree' was blemished from the moment of my birth, *not* because of my colour, but because of the callous indifference of the woman who gave me life.

I am therefore extremely sensitive about how I see myself. In this respect, I should like it clearly understood that I look upon *myself* as being either coloured or 'half-caste'. I am comfortable with either description!

ACKNOWLEDGEMENTS

To:

Greece – the country and her people in general – and to my wonderful extended families in particular for their love and nurturing over the years.

Dr M, for the 'prescription'!

Mr Dennis Vine and Mrs Val Clark and the staff at Making Connections, Barnardo's, for their invaluable help and support throughout the writing of this book.

The Samaritans and Childline for allowing me to use their contact telephone numbers.

The Medici Gallery, for permission to use the picture of Virgin and Child by David.

Messrs Cadburys, for the 'jelly baby' sugar shots that were so indispensable!

Stephen Rhodes, for his beautiful, soothing music.

Jade, for her initial, and well-written, report on my synopsis.

De Deering, who kept me singing!

Jiffy, Joyce, Shana, Ricky, Tessa, Steph, Olive, Major Lesley, Mandy, Jerry and Toni, for their friendship.

Kiran Vyas of Insight Opticians, West Hampstead, for his constant encouragement.

Nickel Press, Seven Kings, Ilford, for their hard work and commendable patience.

CHAPTER ONE

PART I: NAME THIS CHILD!

Away in a manger, no crib for a bed …
Be near me, Lord Jesus; I ask Thee to stay
Close by me forever, and love me, I pray.
                                        ANONYMOUS

The Lord has indeed kept His promise to "stay by my side", although it has taken me years to realise this great truth.

Notwithstanding this, I shall endeavour to commence my story as close to it's beginning as possible.

Unfortunately, no details of my having been either christened or baptised appear on Barnardo's records. However, once I was taken into care, I was baptised into the Church of England.

Let me tell you the name I was known by in Dr Barnardo's Village Home at Barkingside. The surname was *awful* and caused me endless trouble; it was… PLUMB. My name was Susan Jane Plumb.

It was only in 1995, when I was given access to my records, that found out that I had been given the surname of Florence Hammond, who had married a man called Plumb. This was the woman who eventually gave birth to me.

I am aware that when a married woman has a child, the father is assumed to be her husband. This is a point of law. However, since 'Mrs P' knew that she would be having nothing more to do with me once I had been taken into care by Dr Barnardo's, I think it would have been more honest of her to have at least informed them that she would like to have me registered in her maiden name of Hammond.

Having a peculiar name is fine if one is part of a close-knit, loving family. It takes the edge off any laughs that may be had at one's expense. I was already at a disadvantage on two major counts: illegitimate and 'coloured'. I did not need the additional drawback of having to fight my way through years of name-calling, both by children and adults. The fact that I was also called names like Little Black Sambo and Epaminondas (both names of contemporary cartoon characters) and Darkie when I first went to 'outside' school, did not bother me half so much as the constant adaptations of my detested surname. Plums and Custard, Plum Pie, Fruity Plum etc etc *all* were hateful, but had to be endured.

But, the reader might ask, "Would your life have been any different if you *had* been called Hammond?" Most decidedly so: I could have disappeared into the crowd, so to speak. Instead, I grew up to be a child who constantly felt the need to 'show off' and play the clown – what would nowadays be called 'a kid with attitude'.

In 1964 a workmate in my office in Bristol suggested that I change my name to Hamilton. She used to nickname me Lady Hamilton because she said I "put on so many airs"! I took her advice and felt free at last. I am only surprised that I waited so long to do this.

WHAT *IS* IN A NAME?
See the little brown girl running down the street,
With her pretty curls and her clothes so neat.
"Hello there, Darkie!" (She was called so many names
that she'd learnt to laugh them off or not join in any games.)

Her Christian name from day to day she scarcely ever heard;
And, as she grew, the nicknames became much more absurd.

To make things worse, her surname was funny;
She'd change it, she knew, if she had lots of money!
They *all* made jokes – children, and grown-ups too;
It hurt her so much, but what could she *do*?
"Oh, I know! Fight back and pretend that I just don't care;
I'll show off and be naughty; yes I *will*, so there!"

PART II: THE EARLY YEARS

JESUS, friend of little children,
Be a friend to me…
WALTER JOHN MATHAMS (1853–1931)

Trying to fit together my early years is as difficult for me as trying to complete a jigsaw that has no picture on the front of the box. A piece here, a piece there; no safe 'border' to work within. However, I will do the best I can.

I was born on the 2nd of April 1945 and Dr Barnardo's took me 'into care' during August 1946. Apparently no records exist of my life previous to this date. I was placed in Oakley House, which was situated in Frilford Heath, a small village near Abingdon in Berkshire. It was opened on the 15th of March 1946.

Oakley House

With regard to the state of my health at the time of admission into Oakley House, there appears to be some confusion. In one report I read that I was "a healthy child". However, this cannot be the case. According to the Village matron in my second cottage I was in a pretty poor physical condition as a baby. I had ringworm of the scalp, intestinal worms, and was generally undernourished. It also appears that I spent a great deal of time going in and out of hospital, which was the John Radcliffe Infirmary in Oxford.

My earliest recollection is of receiving sun-ray treatment. I 'see' myself sitting on a tiny wooden chair, clad only in a pair of bulky knickers and wearing large heavy spectacles. There are several other children present. We are in a semicircle, facing a huge bright light, which is glowing like the sun. To add point to this 'seaside' effect, we are each holding either a small bucket or a spade, and there is a sprinkling of sand on the floor at our feet!

The scene shifts, and I am standing in a queue, mouth open, apprehensive, waiting to be dosed with one or another of the many 'supplements' it appeared I was in need of. For years afterwards a continuous stream of regulation orange juice, vile-tasting syrup of figs, and lip-smackingly delicious scarlet Parrish's Food – an iron tonic – was spooned into my mouth, and performed their task of building me up. Later on, malt extract was added to the nutritional arsenal. This last was to get me into a great deal of trouble… later on.

Probably as a result of being undernourished as a baby, I was left with defective eyesight, 'fits' and flat feet, which have remained triumphantly flat in spite of constant remedial exercises such as rolling them backwards and forwards on slippery bottles!

In trying to piece together my life before I went to school I am indeed 'clutching at broken straws'. However, I now know that I must have spent quite some time, during this early development, in front of a camera. I know this because when my file was opened I was handed several photographs of myself and other pre-school children. According to a retired Barnardo photographer, we children were photographed in order to raise funds for the Home. Even now, I do not feel that this was a bad

thing, but I should like to have had access to these pictures before I left the Village. When I was first handed them, after a lapse of almost forty years, I felt as though I was looking at a stranger. Who *was* this child? Why did she look so unhappy in *this* photograph, so merry in *that* one? I can vaguely recall that one dress I was wearing at the time of being photographed was mauve Viyella, but that was almost certainly because someone in the Cottage had described it to me later on.

My favourite photograph is this one. As you can see, I was, even at this early stage in my life, a born exhibitionist!

Conductor

PERFORMANCE

Look at my curtsey!
Aren't I just fine!
The band are all waiting –
The audience is *mine*!

I'm in control;
I hold the baton.
Don't boss me about,
I *hate* to be 'sat on'!

Don't move an inch!
I make the rules;
You play when *I* say;
I don't tolerate fools!

Performance is over.
Please clap long and LOUD.
I *love* to be noticed;
To stand out in a crowd!

The only photographs I ever had of myself were either taken at 'outside' school or ones that Village chums and I took of each other after the age of about fourteen. The ones that are shown of me at the seaside were handed to me years after I left the Village; and no colour photographs of me exist before 1964, when I went to Bristol.

I think I was transferred to the Village Home in Barkingside, Ilford just after the severe winter of 1947. The first cottage I was put into was 'Burwell Park', which was situated, first in line, around the Nursery Green, opposite the large asphalt playground of the Village school, Mossford Green. Although I was old enough to leave Oakley House, I could yet not have been entirely fit, as I can recall a great deal of time spent in the Village's isolation hospital. I was about twelve years old before this hospitalisation was discontinued.

The ward was a very lonely place as no one ever visited me. However, I do not recall being unhappy as there were plenty of people around. The lights were on day and night, and I was given one of my favourite foods every day – junket.

I can remember very little more about my early days, except a few incidents concerning my school as an 'infant', and various social events, which will be dealt with in another chapter. Mossford, the Village primary school, was a large, forbidding building with cavernous halls and classrooms on three floors. These floors were made of large, knotty pine planks which threw up clouds of dust as we clattered over them. It catered for children up to, I think, the age of eleven, but I left at seven years of age.

Mossford School

Teaching consisted of the 'Three Rs': reading, 'riting' and 'rithmetic'. I can remember being taught how to knit as 'hand crafts' were part of the school curriculum, and I became very adept in a short time at what was eventually to become a lifetime hobby. The teachers were extremely strict and corporal punishment was the norm, even for very young children. Punishable offences included not doing lessons properly; being cheeky, which was to become my 'speciality' almost from day one; bullying; and running scrunchily up and down the enormous coke pile, which was situated adjacent to the outside boiler room at the back of the school. It was usually only the 'big' boys who committed this heinous crime. However, I can recall being caught by the school caretaker on more than one occasion, and being soundly spanked.

I was also punished for… drinking puddle water and eating worms, although I am now certain that I was 'dared' to do these things by older boys and girls. Another forbidden joy was playing on the revolving TB wards in the grounds of the isolation hospital, at the other end of the Village. These had been used during the First World War by servicemen who had been injured at the Front. The older children used to set these hefty constructions in motion and then jump on, having plonked us younger ones well to the back first. If Matron came along, slappings were dished out all round. The huts were removed in 1957.

TB chalet

Just before I was sent to 'outside' school, I was moved to Heartsease Cottage on the Reception Green. This was, as its name suggests, usually reserved for new arrivals to the Village, and I never learnt the reason for my move there. This was where my *real* fight for survival was to begin. Ironically, heartsease are my favourite flowers!

I was placed in the charge of Miss 'C' and Miss 'D', whom the girls in those days called 'Mum'. At no time ever was *I* permitted to use this title.

I cannot remember why this was so, but it certainly did not auger well for the future, although of course I did not know this at the time.

In many of the cottages, children could use the matrons' Christian names: Aunty Mabel or Aunty Vera. This sounded so much better than the Miss C and Miss D that I was forced to use.

And so, there it was; two major events had already occurred in my short life. I had been transferred to another cottage, and I was being sent to an 'outside the Village' school.

In retrospect, I feel certain that if my needs had been sympathetically met at this early stage in my life, a significant amount of distress could have been avoided. I will endeavour to explain myself more clearly. Whilst I was very young I was 'put out for adoption' on at least three occasions. Needless to say, I had no choice in the matter. I was bathed – no scented soap or talcum powder used in those days, just carbolic and a rough towelling down. My dark, curly locks had a comb drawn painfully through them. Even during those early post-war years of 'austerity' all Barnardo children were beautifully dressed, so I must have looked very pretty in my good quality frock and sandals, and warm woollen coat and beret if the weather was cool. After Matron had inspected me, she would say sharply, "And make sure you behave yourself!"

I was collected, very much like a parcel, by an 'aunty' and 'uncle'. I can vaguely recall being driven long distances and finding myself amongst a crowd of total strangers. I was stared at and followed by children who had almost certainly never set eyes on a coloured child before. However, I was never kept long at these places. According to the matrons, I was sent back to the Village almost immediately for "bad behaviour". Apparently, I started to spit and wet the bed – two things I *never* did in the Cottage! On one occasion, which is forever etched upon my memory, I remember that I had been given a little brown shoulder bag to complete my 'toilette'. This was during Barnardo's last attempt to have me adopted, and I must have been about eight years old. I loathed bags and other girlie trappings such as the ghastly 'Shirley Temple' bows that used to be forcibly tied in my hair. So, right in the middle of the village street (somewhere in Wiltshire, I was told later), I swung the hated bag round and round my head until the strap broke! Actually, I might have been trying to keep name-calling children away from me. Summary punishment was administered upon my return to the Village. I was not put out again for adoption, although I was to be sent on school holidays with another 'aunt' and 'uncle; but more of that later.

Upon reflection, I think that my bizarre behaviour simply stemmed from my childish, natural reaction to being forced into a strange environment amongst people I felt uneasy with. On the surface, I was well-dressed and reasonably attractive; but "You like me when I'm good; let's see if you like me when I'm *BAD!*" Any takers?

I was now about to take my place in the big world outside the Village. I was in a new cottage with new matrons – the youngest 'addition' to a family of growing girls, all of whom were complete strangers to me. Surely this was a daunting prospect for one so young!

CHAPTER TWO:
Parents

PART I: MOTHER (MRS P)

Miss Ophelia: Who was your mother?
Topsy: Never had none.
Miss Ophelia: Never had any mother? What do you
mean? Where were you born?
Topsy: Never was born.
Miss Ophelia: Tell me where you were born and who
your mother and father were.
Topsy: Never was born ... I s'pect I grow'd.

From Uncle Tom's Cabin by
Mrs HARRIET BEECHER STOWE (1811–96)

And there you have it. I was to wait for over forty years before I became any wiser than poor Topsy. When I eventually came into possession of my birth certificate, I found that the entry under 'father' was a false one. I was registered on the 9th of April 1945 at Hitchin, Hertfordshire. What happened to me during the sixteen-month period I presumably spent in Mrs P's care, I was never to discover. As far as I know, I had indeed just 'grow'd'!

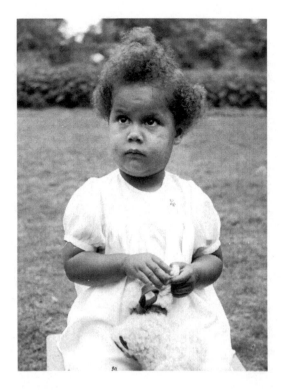

The earliest photographs taken at Frilford Heath show a reasonably healthy-looking little girl dressed in a pretty frock. However, when I first saw these pictures I cried, because the expression on my face is one no child should ever wear. I look harassed and my complexion is blemished. There are deep worry lines across my forehead. I find these images, even today, deeply disturbing considering the pictures were taken at least two full years after having been taken into care by Dr Barnardo's. And indeed, they are in curious contrast to photographs taken a year or so further on. Am I *really* the same little girl or, had a mix-up occurred when my file was being dealt with?

When I was about eight years old, I started to have 'petit mal' attacks. In fact, I might have been suffering from them at an earlier stage, but not been aware of them. They often used to occur when I was standing at the tops of flights of stairs. There would be a cry and a thud, followed by a 'bumpety bump' as my little body tumbled down the stairs. According to eyewitnesses, I automatically rolled myself into a ball. No injuries were caused, but I *can* recall feeling somewhat dazed! I was given Luminal for several years – something which I understand was the only treatment available at that time. Later on, I was told that these attacks had developed after I had recovered from an attack of whooping cough.

Mrs P took no interest in me throughout the years I spent in the care of Barnardos and, in retrospect, the only thing I can be grateful to her for is for producing me on the second and not on the first of April!

Incidentally, there were to be no real 'mother' figures in my life until I went to Greece in 1974. There, the words *mamma, manna* and *manoula* came naturally to me after a very short period, and this has remained the case up to the present time.

FOOTNOTE

Whilst I was writing the above, a Barnardo worker in the Making Connections Department handed me several papers that had been overlooked when my file was in the process of preparation prior to being passed over to me. The papers had been folded before being placed in an envelope.

At first, I was too nervous to investigate. Then one day, I plucked up my courage and took these papers out of their envelope... to be faced with a copy letter that caused me such distress that I shuffled the lot back into the envelope and put them at the bottom of my filing box.

Recently, however, I decided that if I were to write a *full* account of my life in Dr Barnardo's, I would need to make acquaintance with any and *all* information that I had been given.

With much trepidation, therefore, I separated the papers and read them at one sitting. I give below, not the letter referred to above, which is not appropriate to the chapter, but Dr Barnardo's report upon my being admitted into their care on the aforesaid 19th of March 1946.

(For my younger readers, I should perhaps explain that when a female, single or married, 'got into trouble' in those days, it was called a 'lapse'!) Certain portions of this report have been omitted as they do not concern me, and I have substituted the word 'woman' for 'mother'.

QUOTE:
BORN: 2.4.45 at Hitchin Hospital – not baptised. The woman (36) health fairly good; general character: usually good...

HALF-CASTE CHILD
The woman has no near relatives living. ... Married on the 12th of December 1931. ... There are no children of the marriage, and it is reported that the woman was reluctant to bear children because ... she had a fear of INHERITED EPILEPSY [author's capitals] though it has not been revealed from which source this might evolve.

While her husband was serving in the RAF, the woman associated with a coloured American, by whom she gave birth to Susan.

The ... father is stated to be a well-educated man. He was married and the woman did not correspond with him after she became pregnant...

The woman has made several untruthful statements concerning Susan in order to keep her lapse a secret. On the child's birth certificate the woman's husband is represented as being the father of Susan.

When eventually Susan was placed with a foster mother, the woman TOLD HER NEIGHBOURS AND FRIENDS THAT THE CHILD HAD DIED [author's capitals].

Husband ... has been told of the circumstances of Susan's birth and he has forgiven the woman for her lapse, but he has refused to allow the child to remain in his home.

It had been decided to admit Susan when a vacancy can be found for her, and the woman has already signed an agreement (22nd of March). Meanwhile a grant of £1. 5s. 0d. per week had been made in respect of the child while she remains in the care of the foster mother.
UNQUOTE

I leave it entirely up to my readers to imagine how I felt after reading the above, and I ask them not to judge me too harshly when, after I had left the Village, I flatly refused to be reunited with this woman (and at *that* time, I was only angry at her for not having had any contact with me).

This proposed reunion will be referred to in a later chapter.

To conclude, I harbour no resentment whatever towards the woman's husband. His refusal to recognise me was natural, bearing in mind that I was not his own child and that I was coloured. Very few men, even in today's society, would be willing to forgive an adulterous wife such a lapse, regardless of the child's colour.

PART II – FATHER

Praise my soul, the king of Heaven ...
Father-like, He tends and spares us,
Well our feeble frame He knows;
In His hands He gently bears us,
Rescues us from all our foes.
HENRY FRANCIS LYTE (1793–1847)

Reader, before I commence this part of my story, I want you to pause. Now think of the *one* word that gives you the greatest feeling of pleasure. THE word that acts as the 'Open Sesame!' to your consciousness of loving and being loved; of being held close and feeling secure. Well? I trust I have at least started you thinking things over.

The Open Sesame! for me has always been the word: FATHER.

From the time I was first able to give my thoughts substance, I have longed for a father. No doubt to some readers all this may look rather over-sentimental, but, to quote Sophia from *The Golden Girls*, "Picture the scene...!"

It is Open Day in the Village and I am in attendance, smartly dressed. A daring motorcycle team has been invited to display its skills, and... look! The Dagenham Girl Pipers swing onto the Big Green, dazzling my eyes with their impeccable uniforms and making me sway to their stirring music! The sun is shining and people who live outside the Village have brought their families with them to join in the fun. You might think everyone is happy, including me. Really? Think again!

OPEN DAY

'They' let me stand on the edge of the Green and look
At the people; the families. I remember the book
That I held in my hands;
It was *The Faraway Tree*.
Oh! how I longed and longed to be
Whisked off to an exciting, magical land.
But, whilst I was here on earth I could see
That there really was no place for me.

The children chattered and laughed; their faces glowed in the sun.
Some ran to their fathers and were swung high in the fun.
(In *my* Magic Land, Daddy would do just the same.
He'd never tease me; he'd use my *real* name!)

'They' said I could watch if I didn't "make my presence known".
I was good. I looked. I smiled. I sighed and felt... so ALONE!
I was dressed nicely, pushed forward and yet, held back.
People would ask who I was ("What a sweet little black!")

'They' would say "Yes, she does look pretty, but don't be taken in
By those soft, dark eyes and the honey-coloured skin.
She's not like the others, has to be *trained*;
At the end of the day, we feel... quite drained!"
I stood and listened; I'd heard it all before.
I looked down at my arms and legs, and was sure
That the reason I had no father was because I was brown.
("A darkie with *your* background must be kept down!")

I shuffled my feet and gazed up at the sun;
The Open Day was ruined, my pleasure quite gone.
'They' told me all was over; the 'fun' was at an end.
My aching eyes searched the empty Green...
                    for a father and a friend!

Open days, or fetes, as they were usually called, were held in order to raise funds for Dr Barnardo's, and a very good idea they were too. Visitors could look round the Village and sometimes a particular cottage would be singled out for visit by a well-known 'personality'. I always felt as if I, too, was 'on show', and cannot say that I much enjoyed these events although, curious to relate, I am unable to recall a rainy one!

Fathers generally were rarely seen in the Village, apart from the cottage fathers who had their own families with them. I cannot remember one ever coming to visit a child in any cottage I was living in. Neither did I ever hear them mentioned in conversation.

From a very early age, I wanted to know if I had a dad like the children at 'outside' school. The matrons told me nothing, save that I was what was known as a "half-caste, probably Indian", though they must have known at the time that this was not the truth. They did, however, tell me that I had two brothers, Carl and Tony, whom I would see "If you are good". More about these brothers later!

I could work none of this out, however. If I had brothers, where were they? Why couldn't I see them? Were they the same colour as me? ("No; they are white and living with their mother.") If she was *their* mother, why wasn't she mine? Where was my father?

Questions, questions, questions, but never an answer did I receive that I could give credence to, even at that early stage in my life.

On looking back, I realise that it must have been difficult for the matrons to deal with the unpleasant subject of bastardy. However, I *do* feel that a suitably unequivocal explanation could have been given to me at, say, the age of eleven, when I would have been capable of understanding at least some of the problems surrounding my birth, and why it had been necessary for me to be taken into care. It would have saved much subsequent emotional turmoil.

The way I dealt with the problem of not being like 'normal' children and having a dad was inevitable. Always an imaginative child – an avid reader of stories such as Enid Blyton's 'Famous Five' (I was George, of course!), Lucy Fitch Perkins charming 'Twins' tales, and Louisa May Alcott's March family saga – I created my *own* 'family'.

No mother, no sisters – just two brothers and a splendid father. At first I was unable to conjure up an ideal father figure, not having had any experience. Then, joy of joys, the films came to Dr Barnardo's! It was decreed that certain well-chosen films would be shown on Saturdays in Mossford School.

A buzz of excitement must have gone round the cottages, and I can assure you that at least *one* little girl did her best not to forfeit her chance of attending the matinees by misbehaving too close to Saturdays!

We filed into the Main Hall, were shown to the sloping tiers of wooden seats and exhorted to "sit down and be *quiet!*" The lights were switched off, the screen flickered with strange black upside-down letters and figures, and we were off!

In those far-off days, everything was black and white. Pathé News first, with its rooster cock-a-doodle-dooing his introduction. This would have been carefully 'edited' by the Village powers-that-be. Then came the main feature, which was usually a Tarzan, Lassie or cowboys-and-indians film. There might also be a Mickey Mouse cartoon, if we were lucky.

I don't know about the other children, but *my* favourite films were the ones starring Richard Widmark. He was a revelation to me from the first. At last I had found my ideal 'father'! Tall, fair, with blue eyes and a warm 'you-will-be-safe-with-*me*' persona, it is no surprise to me, even now, that I chose him, although of course I was not fully aware of the emotional ramifications of my attraction to him. I was also too young to appreciate the impossibility of having such a dashing blond for a father.

I told no one of this fantasy of mine; I hugged it to myself. It was to prove a great comfort to me in times of isolation and unhappiness later on. Some readers might be inclined to ask "But didn't you ever think your father might have been black?" or "Wouldn't you have preferred a black father?" My answer to both questions is "No".

In those days, the stigma of being coloured was enormous. To a sensitive child such as I was, even entering a roomful of white people could be an excruciatingly painful experience. I usually felt it necessary to put on an act of not caring by swaggering about and... making faces!

To have to acknowledge a black father would have been unthinkable. The fact that he might have been kind and loving simply did not enter into the picture. Richard Widmark, then, was to be a 'dream father', my emotional 'sheet anchor', for a number of years; at least until I left the Village;

In the mid-eighties, I decided to change my name again... to WIDMARK!

I should state at this point that, just as in the case with the husband of Mrs P, who refused to accept me, I have never blamed the man who was at least half responsible for my coming into the world.

I have now discovered his name, rank and military number. However, I have no interest in finding out about any of his relations. It is a case of 'Let the past bury the past'. He died in 1963. The details were given to me during the eighties, but, according to my informant, "All other details were lost in a fire..."

The well-known Irish songwriter, William 'Percy' French (of 'Abdul Abulbul Amir' fame) once said of himself, "I was born a child, and have remained a child ever since". This somewhat wistful self assessment could, I think, be aptly applied to me. In spite of my sixty-odd years, the part of me that has always longed for a father has kept alive an almost childlike quality in me that has proved both an emotional and spiritual safeguard over the years.

I have much to be grateful for, to the true FATHER, who has been my strength, and stayed by my side throughout a turbulent life, although I have not always acknowledged His presence!

CHAPTER THREE:
Holidays

Summer suns are glowing,
Over land and sea...
.....
And when clouds are drifting
Dark across our sky,
Then, the veil uplifting,
Father, be thou nigh.
WILLIAM WALSHAM HOW (1823–97)

PART I: A PARADOX

My later chapter entitled 'Everyday Life in the Village' will deal with, amongst other things, what went on during the holidays. However, I have chosen to devote a separate chapter to those holidays which were either the most memorable, or which were to prove of particular significance in my life.

During the years I spent in the Village, many of us children were the victims of a curious paradox. This needs to be clearly explained if the reader is to understand what prompted me to draw especial attention to it. Most of us suffered from some sort of emotional instability, although we lived in a secure environment. We enjoyed 'privileges' that were denied to many 'normal' children, whilst fighting our own personal battles against loneliness and isolation.

PART II: CHRISTMAS AND EASTER

The public was always generous to Dr Barnardo children, and never more so than at Christmas and Easter.

My earliest memories of Christmas are of going to huge parties outside the Village. When I was very young, the most thrilling party I can remember attending was one held at the American Air Force base in West Ruislip. The journey itself was exciting, although it certainly took longer than it would have nowadays as there were no motorways.

The party was held in an aircraft hangar. It was noisy, it was fun, and the trestle tables groaned with all sorts of 'luxury' foods which would have been unavailable to ordinary British families during that period of post-war austerity.

We were given incredible gifts, too. For the boys: baseball bats, helmets and gloves. The girls received beautiful dollies, complicated American games, and boxes of paints.

I do not know about the rest of the children, but I can vaguely recall being told to "be *polite*; eat what you like, but pocket nothing!" I immediately disobeyed the last part of this order by cramming two cream cakes into the frilly pockets of my best party frock!

Needless to say, all our 'hosts' were white. Apparently no coloured officers were to be present at the party. I learnt, many years later, that black personnel were housed in separate billets. At that time, I had no idea whatever that black people played any part in the War. I have no doubt, however, that the fathers of some of us half-caste children were on the base at the time. Mine certainly was, as I discovered after my file had been officially opened and presented to me.

Factories such as Tate & Lyle in London's docklands, and Ford's of Dagenham also used to invite Barnardo children to their Christmas parties later on, and these were much enjoyed by the children who had been fortunate enough to receive an invitation.

On Christmas mornings we were not given the traditional stockings. Instead, pillowcases were filled to the brim with toys and sweets.

Oh, how excited I became when my name was called out, and I grabbed my pillowcase with trembling fingers! The distribution of our gifts would not take place until after breakfast, if I remember correctly, and I know a great deal of thought went into the filling of *my* pillowcase, as I always got what I wanted. First, a large box of Winsor & Newton paints; followed by a painting book; cut-out-and-dress paper dollies; knitting wool; and a toy shop with a 'real' ring-up till, scales and plenty of tiny bottles filled with sweeties. In addition to this bounty, we all received fruit. If we were *very* lucky, an orange would be stuffed into a corner of a pillowcase. In the early fifties, this fruit was considered a luxury.

Another treat at Christmas was the West End pantomime. As with the big outside parties, cottages attended these pantomimes 'by rote' each year. Let me tell you about the two most memorable of these. I was among the lucky youngsters who benefited from an error, and what an unforgettable experience it proved to be! One year, a mistake was made by the Village office. The younger children should have gone to a pantomime (I think it was *Snow White*) and the older girls had been invited to see the enchanting *Where the Rainbow Ends*. Valentine Dyall was one of the principal actors, as I recall. I think he played a demon.

However, the pantomime that thrilled me the most one year was *Cinderella*. As usual, our Barnardo contingent was admitted through a side entrance and shown to our seats. The curtain rose and poor Cinders was revealed, sitting pensively by the fire. She was played by a beautiful 'star' called Yana, whose name, we were told later, was an acronym for Yet Another National Asset! I wonder what became of her?

The actor who most delighted me, however, was the new young 'discovery' who played Buttons. He was to become my very first pop idol later on. Blond and cheeky, with an effervescent singing style that we little girls found irresistible, Tommy Steele truly 'ran away with the show'!

I was told later on that the Barnardo children had all gone backstage to meet him after the pantomime, but I do not remember this; shame on me!

Easter was the second most important event in our Village 'church calendar'. As far as I was concerned though, it usually meant "Will I like my new clothes" and "How many Easter eggs will I get!" For some inexplicable reason, I always had a new frock and shoes at this time, at least during the earlier years.

With Matron striding beside us, we girls were marched off to the big clothing stores, next to the school. This was run by a wonderful lady who was gentle and patient with the children. Miss 'Y' had been a heroine in the last war. We heard that she had rescued some children from a fire in the Blitz, getting dreadfully burnt during the process. Her face and arms were permanently scarred, but I do not remember any child ever making fun of her. We had been told her story at a very early age and I, for one, was proud and fond of her.

So, Easter morning had arrived! Each cottage sets off to church; the bells are ringing out a simple Easter hymn. We are walking along in a 'crocodile' formation, accompanied by both matrons and maybe an assistant trainee matron. As with Christmas, I was on my best behaviour, barring the occasional lapse into staring around me. The reason for this enforced 'being good' was that I knew my eggs would not be given to me if I was naughty. In addition, I would not be in line, literally, for the extra-special treat.

Every Easter, Fortes (the well-known restaurant chain) sent an enormous decorated egg to the Village. Across the front of this egg was emblazoned "Happy Easter from Fortes!" It was accompanied by a number of large boxes which contained smaller eggs. The egg was photographed, with children and nursery nurses, after which it was taken away, broken up and distributed among the cottages. The chocolate chunks were very thick and utterly delicious; yum yum! But, mind, only for the well-behaved! I can recall going without on at least two dismal occasions.

Fortes Easter egg

PART III: SUMMER FUN

During the summer holidays, each cottage spent two weeks by the sea. The resort allotted to the cottages I lived in was Clacton-on-Sea. (My best chum went to Birchington.)

Oh, what fun it was getting ready for the journey! The big open-backed army lorry was packed with boxes of food, bedding and clothing. We smaller 'fry' were stowed safely away in the middle with the matrons, while the lucky big girls clung precariously onto the backboard – no Health & Safety meddling in *those* halcyon days! There was no 'motorway madness' either – just a long, thrilling ride through delightfully unspoilt countryside. As we drove through small towns and villages, passers-by would be saluted with happy waves. Arrived at Clacton, we were housed in a large building that seemed to consist of one long dormitory, with a bathroom extension branching off it. The kitchen and dining room were located in a smaller, separate building in the grounds. Here is a photograph of me, taken on Clacton promenade. In the background is the pier with its 'Steel Stella' switchback, which I know the big girls went on although I would have been too young for this treat. I do remember, however, incurring a very painful graze whilst going down the large helter-skelter slide on a piece of coconut matting.

Clacton 1950s

In this photograph, I am wearing a nondescript, washed-out swimsuit of blue, which had become extremely 'felted' from frequent dips in the sea. I am tall, leggy, deeply tanned and boyish looking. My flat feet are very evident, too!

One of the *really* naughty things I used to do at Clacton, but only when the matrons or big girls were not in sight, was to hitch my swimsuit up at the back, between my little brown buttocks, pre-dating today's objectionable 'thong' by many a long year! I do not know why I did this, although it *did* raise a few eyebrows I can tell you, as I trotted along the 'prom'. Occasionally, I would jump down onto the beach and weave in and out of the crowded deckchairs. Voices would be raised crossly as I tripped over picnic baskets or knocked down carefully constructed sandcastles, but I don't recall anyone ever grabbing hold of me. Maybe I was too nippy to ever be caught!

In retrospect, I can only assume this to have been one of my many and varied attention-grabbing exercises.

Butlins holiday camp had not long been opened at Clacton, and the older girls used to be allowed to go there during the day. Non-residents did not have to pay in those days, and on one happy occasion I was taken to the roller skating rink by two of the big girls. What fun I had, once the skates were strapped onto my white canvas beach shoes, even though I spent most of the time on my bottom!

On Sundays, we did not attend church, but sat decorously on the sand and joined in the Salvation Army beach services. I always used to feel sorry for the 'Soldiers' in their dark, hot-looking uniforms, caps and bonnets. I liked watching the officer in charge flipping over the large sheets of paper on which popular hymns and choruses had been printed. The big brass instruments glittered in the sun as young and old joined in to sing happily such old favourites as 'Eternal Father Strong to Save' and 'Blessed Assurance, Jesus is Mine!'

When I was recuperating from one or the other of my childhood maladies, I used to be sent to Barnardo convalescent homes at either Great Yarmouth in Norfolk, or Deal in Kent. These 'holidays' were not much fun as they took place during the off seasons. I remember an incident when I almost drowned at Great Yarmouth. Some local boys were shooting arrows into the air. Suddenly, one of the arrows changed course and flew out to sea. Underneath my regulation navy raincoat I was wearing a swimsuit, so I volunteered to brave the very choppy sea in order to retrieve it. However, at that time I did not have any idea just how deceptive perspective can be! I disappeared from view several times before I was able to reach the arrow. The sea was very rough, and the return journey seemed interminable. I swallowed great mouthfuls of salt water as I dog-paddled my way back to the shore. The onlookers were extremely distressed as they dragged me, spluttering and bedraggled, from Neptune's playground. In those days there were no lifeguard lookout posts. Nor do I ever remember seeing any first-aid stations on promenades. I don't think we were ever accompanied by 'responsible adults' either.

One of the favourite beach games enjoyed by Barnardo children was 'skipping stones', or 'ducks and drakes', as it was usually called. Yarmouth beach was dangerously sloping and pebbly. The older boys used to place the small children on the lower level of the beach, whilst they showed off their skills behind us. Sometimes there were accidents, and to this day I still have a large bony lump at the back of my skull where a badly thrown pebble struck me. I was knocked out cold, and only regained consciousness some hours later in our dormitory. How I was transported there, or by whom, I have never known, though I *do* remember the name of the dormitory: it was Windjammer!

I cannot recollect the exact year when cottage holidaying ended, for me, at any rate. It might have been 1956, when I went up to secondary school. All I *do* know is that the discontinuing of the cottage holidays turned out to be a terrible mistake on Barnardo's part, although the results would not become evident for a few years.

Because I had no family, I was allotted an 'aunty' and 'uncle', with whom I was to spend part of the summer holidays. No prior notice was given to me, and it goes without saying that I was not consulted in the matter. Neither was I given the opportunity of meeting them first to see if we liked each other. I was simply informed that from such-and-such a date I would be writing to my new aunty and uncle.

It never occurred to me to question how or why I had been 'selected', or by whom. I can only assume that the aunty and uncle had visited the Village previously and picked me out of a crowd of youngsters. Upon mature consideration, I am certain that I was picked out *because* I was coloured and looked different! The couple who chose me came from a small town in the West Country, where the appearance on the streets of a dark-skinned child would cause a sensation. Many times I have asked myself the question, "Why couldn't they have opted for a white girl or boy, who would have had a much greater chance of fitting in to their lifestyle?" This is indeed that 64,000-dollar question which has never been answered.

I do not think too much blame should be cast on Dr Barnardo's, as they were only trying to act in my best interests. I rather think that my two matrons had approached the office and mentioned that they were not willing to include me in the cottage holidays any more. This might seem rather incomprehensible to the reader at present, but all will be revealed further on.

The holidays I spent with the new aunty and uncle were marvellous once I had recovered from the ghastly journey, which was mostly undertaken on the old A4. The couple would collect me from our cottage in a tiny, grey Austin Seven. I wonder how many older readers remember these! I was always terribly car sick, occasioning frequent stops along the way.

Upon arrival, I was introduced to the respective families (I liked uncle's best!) and made much of. I must have caused quite a stir in that part of the world: I looked so *very* different from everyone else. I was much darker than I am today and at the 'all-arms-and-legs' stage. I spoke rapidly in a racy semi-Cockney dialect, which was a complete contrast to the slower and broader West Country burr. I was often laughingly told to repeat myself or just "speak more *slowly*"!

These were the golden days before foreign holidays became the norm. We usually set off, in two or three family cars, for places such as Minehead, Weston-super-Mare or Cheddar in Somerset; or Torquay, Seaton and Instow in Devon. The journeys were often so far flung that we 'bed-and-breakfasted', which was a new and exciting experience for me. Wherever I went I was the centre of attraction; one simply did not meet with coloured children, or adults, in those days. To add to this crowd-drawing effect, I was always well-dressed in pretty frocks (which I loathed!) or Aertex blouses and box-pleated shorts. I also wore beautifully knitted 'cardies' and jumpers that aunty, her sisters or her mother presented to me.

On one of my holidays, I was permitted to bring another Barnardo girl with me. I chose Mary, a girl of my own age and colour. We were both at that age when looks were becoming important, and we amused aunty and uncle by appearing at the breakfast table in shimmering green eyeshadow and... lipstick! These would almost certainly have been Rimmel products, bought in either Woolworths or Boots, as they were the cheapest on the market at that time, and holiday pocket money did not go far!

These holidays meant a great deal to me as I now had a 'family' I could boast of when I returned to school in September.

The magic only ended when something happened that I had not been adequately prepared for. It occurred whilst we were at the seaside in Somerset. It was sudden and frightening. The aunties hustled me off to the public conveniences and 'fixed me up'. When we returned to the family, 'my' aunty informed the men that "Susan has become a woman!" It was a deeply embarrassing moment for everyone, including the men. I know that even her own sisters were annoyed at her insensitivity. She later told me that I must be *extra* careful about washing, as I would "smell more than white girls".

The holidays were over for me... in more ways than one.

CHAPTER FOUR:
Everyday Life In The Village

Lead us, Heavenly Father, lead us
O'er the world's tempestuous sea;
Guard us, guide us, keep us, feed us
For we have no help but Thee.
Yet possessing every blessing
If our God our Father be.
JAMES EDMESTON (1791–1867)

PART I: OUR VILLAGE AND ITS BENEFACTOR

Just how much *I* was being led by our Heavenly Father will, I trust, become clearer to the reader as my story unfolds.

However, our earthly 'father' was very much a presence in all our young lives. There were pictures of him everywhere, and we were brought up to respect and, in theory anyway, love him... As our benefactor...

Thomas John Barnardo was born in Dublin in 1845. His family were of Jewish descent, but he became a Christian and spent his entire life helping underprivileged children. He was a man of great warmth and compassion. His tragically early death, at the age of sixty, was caused chiefly by overwork on behalf of 'his' children.

Thomas John Barnardo

The children's home at Barkingside, Ilford, Essex was officially opened in 1876. It was originally called The Girls' Village Home, and the initials GVH were painted in large white letters on the water tank of the Village laundry. They were visible for miles around. During my time in the Village, these letters were changed to TVH – The Village Home.

When I arrived in the Village, it comprised three main areas: the Nursery, Reception, and Big Greens. There were sixty-four 'cottages' altogether, and various ancillary buildings including an isolation hospital and a dispensary. There was no dental clinic until the late 1950s, which necessitated the children being taken to the nearby boys' home at Woodford Green.

Governor's House GVH

The beautiful 'Governor's House' was the hub of Village administration. This building had cool, tiled halls and walkways, and had been specially designed to accommodate wheelchair users.

When I returned to the Village in later years, I was outraged (as indeed were most of my contemporaries) to find that the Governor's House had been brutally razed to the ground and a hideously inferior construction erected in its place.

I remember one occasion when I was chosen to go to tea with the Colonel and his wife. It was an awe-inspiring experience, and I think I was tongue-tied for most of the time – a rarity for me!

The Colonel and his family were very much of the Old School, what used to be called in earlier years 'the gentry'. Their rule was rather strait-laced but mild, and they were much respected, both by grown-ups and children alike. I often used to see the 'sewing ladies' going in and out of the House. These were women who used to go round to the cottages during the week to do the mending, at which they were experts, having being trained at the embroidery school in the Village.

They wore callipers (leg braces), and were probably the victims of poliomyelitis. In the early fifties, the Salk vaccine was put into general use, and this crippling illness was virtually eradicated.

Embroidery School

The sewing ladies used cumbersome wheelchairs that were driven by a chain and a rotating handle, which steered the front wheel. There were two large rear wheels. Strictly speaking, these chairs were designed for one person only, but sometimes a lucky child would be taken onto one of the ladies' laps and off they would go, on a trip round the Village.

'Our' lady, for some reason I never discovered, (although I did learn that her name was Susan, like mine) disliked me intensely and showed it at all times. This being the case, I was never to find out what it was like to ride in one of these wheelchairs.

Opposite the Governor's House was Cairns, the clock tower building which has fortunately escaped demolition. In it resided Miss 'G', the formidable Village head. She used to cycle all round the Village on her 'sit-up-and-beg' bicycle, with its loud, 'bossy' bell. This bicycle must have made a long-lasting impression upon me, because just over a year ago I bought one like it for myself, complete with the bell!

Cairns and Church

Memorial to Dr Barnardo

Miss G had the eyes of Argus and was always appearing behind us children, but only, it seemed, when we were misbehaving!

Although life inside the cottages was directed by the resident matron and either a co-matron or young trainee 'assistant', the overall control of the Village remained under the tight supervision of the Head Office. During my early years, this was based in the Barnardo building at Stepney Causeway.

This imposing edifice had the words NO DESTITUTE CHILD EVER REFUSED ADMISSION painted across its entire frontage.

I think all my contemporaries at the Village passed through Stepney at some time or other. I can recall being photographed there just before I left the Village, but I will deal with this later on.

The Village was almost completely self-sufficient; it even had its own large orchard. This was off-limits to us children, but what fun we used to have scrumping there! They say that stolen fruits taste the sweetest. I am not so sure about this; I can still feel the griping pains that I experienced after a raid on the orchard with the boys. I would receive no sympathy from the matrons – just an extra punishment such as filling the heavy coke scuttles, which of course added to my agony. Served me right, too!

(Reminiscences of all that went on in the Village are crowding around me so much now, that I am finding it rather difficult to sort them out. I trust therefore that the reader will bear with me, whilst I shuffle through my pack of memory cards and attempt to place them in some sort of order.)

Ah! Yes! We even had our own postal service in the Village. The post vehicle was a large, basket-like contraption with a lid, which was trundled round the cottages twice a day. It was usually pushed by a much-trusted 'big' girl. We children used to rush excitedly to our playroom windows to see if she would stop at *our* cottage. This 'post girl' also brought internal post from the office to the cottage heads.

The letters and parcels, if any, would be handed over for sorting and distribution. I do not know what system other cottages employed, but all *my* letters were read, and parcels opened, before I received them. Up to the time I left Dr Barnardo's I never once received an unopened letter or parcel, and I feel indignant about this even now.

PART II: DUTIES AND ACTIVITIES

Children in the Village were kept occupied at all times. In each cottage there was a system of duties, which was strictly adhered to. Chores such as the aforementioned coke scuttle filling, potato peeling and shoe cleaning were done by older children. The 'little ones' were expected to keep the playroom reasonably tidy and put their toys away in their respective lockers after play. Other jobs included the laying and clearing of tables, and stacking dirty china and cutlery. Washing up was only done by the very reliable.

Mr Dennis Vine, who with his wife had taken over a cottage in 1957, told me that a severe 'regime' had been in force there. Saturday morning jobs would be allocated to each lad. When the job was done, it would be inspected. If all was in order, a fresh job immediately followed! This was a particularly cruel system as it gave the lads no incentive to work properly.

The new master introduced a much more reasonable plan, whereby upon satisfactory completion of his chore, the boy would be handed his 'pocket money' and was free until mealtime. Mr Vine told me recently that "the atmosphere changed immediately and *all* jobs were done well – first time round!"

All Barnardo children were responsible for making their own beds from a very early age, and woe betide sloppy bed makers! In the stricter cottages, their beds would be stripped down, to be remade "before you come down to breakfast!" As soon as we came back from school, we would change into our 'play clothes'.

Our school clothes, in my cottage at any rate, would be carefully brushed and hung up on pegs in the cloakroom, which was just inside the back door. Our shoes would be exchanged for slippers, or 'plimsolls' if we were going out to play. To this day, I maintain that this is an excellent system; I have adhered to it all my life!

After meals, those without chores or homework, and not 'on punishment' (today's young people would call this 'being grounded') could go out to play; and *how* we played!

The big boys made 'jiggers' – soapbox carts which were mounted on old pram wheels. In these, they hurtled round the Village, scaring the daylights out of the smaller children. There were the usual ball games to play against walls, with the girls tucking their frocks into their knickers for the more advanced actions. 'Jacks' and the ancient 'knucklebones' now known as 'five stones' were always popular too. One Christmas, some of us older children received the then-fashionable 'Jacoskates', and spent many painful hours tottering around the school playground until we became confident enough to link hands and glide effortlessly on the pathways, to the envy of our less fortunate playmates.

Later on, bicycles were donated; not many and certainly not 'one per cottage', but they were much appreciated by budding cyclists. The most beautiful cycle I remember was a girls' one called the Pink Witch. It was a lovely, extremely modern, combination of shocking pink and aquamarine. However, I was never lucky enough to ride on one!

As a matter of course, some of us joined Scout and Guide troops, but these were usually held outside the Village, in church halls. My last troop section was called Larkspur, a flower that has remained a favourite of mine over the years. I remember marching towards the Village church. It was a very special occasion called Thinking Day, which I believe has gone out of fashion now. Both boys and girls were responsible for keeping their own uniforms in pristine condition, and I grew to detest the plump yellow ties which were so difficult to knot. How I envy today's youngsters in their snappy, practical outfits!

All sorts of 'classes' were available to Village children. I remember attending ballroom dancing in the Embroidery School. Only the girls took part and we were taught, among other things, the 'social graces':

how to behave at a dance, how to enter a ballroom, etc, and I became quite adept at the art of 'chaseéing' up to my partner and requesting her hand for the Military Two-step or Veleta. We also learnt the energetic 'Gay Gordons' and 'Strip the Willow'. The boys used to cling onto the windowsills and make faces at us, but much *we* cared!

At one time, the Isadora Duncan style of dancing became the fashion for some unknown reason. We girls had to wear short tunics of magenta or forest green, with horribly bulky self-coloured 'bloomers' underneath. Our feet were bare. This dancing would take place on the Big Green, but it was not at all popular and was soon discontinued, thank goodness!

Cricket and hockey were taught by one of the younger masters. I did not like hockey very much because I found it too nerve wracking, and used to go wild at the 'bullying off'. I enjoyed cricket, although I was not much of a batsman. I was, however, a nimble run maker. As usual, I refused to wear my spectacles, so was always put into slip fielding. The most fun we had was when we youngsters played against the masters, and I can still hear our jubilant shouts of Howzat! as one of the boys bowled out a master for a 'duck'!

Archery classes (yes, really!) were held behind Sunshine Court, which is now called Queen Victoria House. In my day this was a peaceful nursery green, which had an elegant gazebo-style shelter on it. Now archery was one sport I should *never* have attempted! Always unpredictable, something of a show-off, and not very amenable to discipline, I proved to be lethal at the butts. It was not long before I was ordered to leave. The classes did not last very long: probably considered too risky for *all* parties concerned.

Sunshine Cottage

Not far from the Big Green, and close to the isolation hospital, was a large play area. It was furnished with a slide, see-saw and swings. These had been set into a macadamised surface. Some of the children used to be able to 'swing up to the sky', which I envied. They took many falls, resulting in all sorts of injuries, and broken 'second' teeth occurred frequently. However, it was all good fun, and any accidents were usually shrugged off. Opposite this play area was the swimming pool. It had remained derelict for some time, probably due to the War. However, in 1957 it was refurbished.

Our sports master, Mr Vine, held the key and supervised its general maintenance, including the times of opening and closing.

On summer evenings it was used by the young nurses and trainee assistant nursery nurses. Although it had a shallow end, deep end and diving platform, it was very basic in design. The cubicles were wooden, and the boys used to swim hopefully past the girls' side and try to catch us changing!

I used to spend most of my time on the springboard, and became quite skilful acrobat on it. The pool would sprout a coating of algae, and later in the year the surface would have to be cleared of the hundreds of leaves which fell from the horse chestnut trees that overhung it.

Mr Vine would see that these leaves were cleared daily before the pool was used. The pool would then be emptied and cleaned. (The boys loved this mucky job!) It was refilled regularly. Each week it would be inspected, treated with harmless chemicals, and tested by Mr Vine and a member of the Village maintenance team. These chemicals would be safely locked away in the maintenance office, which was situated near the laundry.

On Saturdays, we older children were taught life-saving drill by a master who had been an RSM during the War. He was barrel-chested, had a stentorian voice, and was extremely strict. We used to 'muster' at about nine o'clock, regardless of the weather, and stand shivering on the edge of the pool. On the word of command, the carefully segregated rows of boys and girls would plunge into the icy green water. All in all, these classes were enjoyed. We were taught both Holger-Nielson and Schafer life-saving methods; I wonder how many of us Old Boys and Girls have ever been called upon to put our skills into practice over the years. On one very exciting occasion, the Colonel's much-loved dog Susie tumbled into the pool, and had to be rescued by some of the big boys.

These days, of course, our pool would have been closed down due to health and safety reasons, but we loved it, and it gave a great deal of pleasure to both children and grown-ups alike. The only flies in our ointment were the occasional verrucas or outbreaks of athletes foot, to which I became a martyr!

One pool incident remains fixed in my memory. I was with a group of children returning from a swim. Now, I'm not sure *exactly* what I said to one of the girls, who, incidentally, lived in the same cottage as me. It was probably something like 'Fatty' because she was rather plump.

Unfortunately this was overheard by the redoubtable Miss G, who had appeared, as usual, from nowhere. She pedalled up behind me roaring out "Come here, girl! Right NOW!" or words to that effect. I tremblingly obeyed. She took off her leather belt and, using the buckle end, flogged me all the way back to the Cottage as I was forced to trot by her side. As it was roughly a ten-minute run, I was rather sore about the shoulders and back! On arrival at the Cottage, Miss G insisted that I receive further punishment "to teach you a lesson". Ouch!

I learnt, only recently that, even in those days, this would have been considered a criminal act, which witnesses should have reported to the Colonel. 'Corporal punishment' could be used legitimately at that time using:

> … a Home Office-approved cane ONLY. Incidents are to be entered into the Official Punishment Book for Inspectors to examine.

My informant and his wife had worked in other Barnardo homes for five years, so knew these facts. He also said that he "doubted if anyone else in the Village was aware that the Village was a law unto itself". Interesting!

Also in 1957 there was some sort of political upheaval in Hungary, and Barnardo's took in several refugees. They were distributed between the cottages, although our cottage did not receive any. I do not know how long they stayed, but I *do* remember being 'sweet' on a boy called Jan. Needless to say, he was blond and blue-eyed! I heard from other Village children that these youngsters were shy but that they soon settled into their respective cottages. I wonder what became of them all.

The most prestigious occasion as far as sporty children were concerned were the Inter-homes sports, which were held on the Big Green at Barkingside Village. I was passionate about running; it was an excellent outlet for all the excess energy that fizzed up inside me. Several of the masters had been efficient athletes in their colleges or universities, so we children received expert tuition in various disciplines. Practices took place during the lighter evenings after school, and on Saturdays.

Those were the days when Sunday really *was* the day of rest. No sports or outdoor games were permitted. In addition to this, of course, all shops were closed except the newsagents. These were allowed to open in the mornings for the sale of Sunday newspapers and cigarettes. However, I seem to be wandering from my subject!

The trainer I remember with greatest affection was Mr Vine, a comparative newcomer to the Village. He proved to be a rigid but fair disciplinarian, always on the lookout for budding athletes, and I was thrilled to be selected for the hundred-yards and eighty-yards 'dash'.

The golden year for the Village was 1958, when our athletics team won all the track and field awards. How proud we all were as we went up to collect our cups and medals! We were dressed in dazzlingly white Aertex sports shirts with a scarlet V (for Village) sewn across the front. Both boys and girls wore natty white shorts, socks and plimsolls. Spiked running shoes normally reserved for cinder tracks were only worn on our school sports fields in those days, although they were grass. We had all been presented with stylish Bukta tracksuits, which were 'the last word' on sports fields at that time. They had been purchased by the Colonel from public donations to the Village.

The boys used to call me the 'Brown Bomber' because I was such a fast runner. This was a somewhat inappropriate nickname as it was the one used by the world-famous boxer Joe Louis!

There was a tradition in the Village whereby victorious athletes would be given a high tea to celebrate their prowess. These jolly meals took place in the athletes' respective cottages and, I understand, were much enjoyed.

Sports day Dennis Vine & Suzan

Here is a photograph of me, sitting next to our trainer Mr Vine. One does not need to be a qualified child psychologist in order to interpret my rather worrying body language and facial expression. I think I look completely defeated and unhappy. In actual fact, I was both. I knew that however much I achieved on the sports field (and I came first in all my heats as well as the finals), there would be no 'special tea' for *me*. The only comments passed by the matrons in my cottage were "...and so you *ought* to have won, given the amount of food you eat" or "...the enormous sums spent on you"! I can honestly state that the matrons never gave me any encouragement for achievements, either on the sports field or in the classroom. The inevitable result of this, not unnaturally, was that I became over the years a deeply resentful 'non-achiever', whose natural talents were neither recognised nor appreciated.

There was also a thriving netball team in the Village, and I played either centre defence or attack. We were sometimes invited to play outside the Home. On one particular occasion, we went down to the East End to play at the Mayflower Family Centre in Canning Town. This was when the well-known England and Sussex cricketer Reverend David

Sheppard was warden. He was later to become the Bishop of Liverpool. We were driven to the Centre in the Village store's army lorry. As usual, all us girls were correctly dressed in smart box-pleated navy shorts, Aertex shirts and black plimsolls. On this occasion, however, I was not at all satisfied with my appearance; I wanted to wear TIGHT shorts! I have never been able to understand what made me feel this way at that particular time; I was usually painfully self-conscious of my legs! Nevertheless, I persuaded one of the younger girls to 'swap' with me. Her shorts were *so* tight on me that when I got down from the lorry in Canning Town I was forced to walk almost on tiptoe! At lunchtime the team descended on the local market and paraded around the booths showing off our nubile limbs. Goodness me! It is probably just as well that I am quite unable to remember any of the many comments bawled at us by the stallholders!

* * *

Village children were only allowed off the premises at stipulated times, or when accompanied by an adult.

As we grew older, the majority of us naturally became restless about this and often took the law into our own hands. We almost always headed for the old aerodrome near Barkingside Station. Although this had ceased to be used just after the War, the Nissen huts remained. These were occupied by families who had been evacuated from the East End of London. The huts were strictly off-limits to all Barnardo children, so of course we were magnetically drawn towards them! I had been told by 'my' matrons that the families were "low class East Enders"!

Although I was initially shocked at the poor living conditions in the huts, I was vaguely titillated at being accepted as 'one of the crowd'. The huts had huge smelly oil stoves in them, and the 'rooms' were partitioned with some sort of heavy curtaining, which gave minimal privacy. I do not think I ever had any food there. I was, strange though it may seem, a little snobbish and would certainly have turned up what the matrons used to call my 'noble nose' at anything that had been cooked on the primitive equipment!

I think it was also on the aerodrome that I learnt to… climb pylons! I am sure that there were some in those far-off days. This was an exceedingly dangerous undertaking and, of course, should never have been attempted; but it was the result of a 'dare', and my pride was at stake. Another enjoyable spree was to jump on and off the Martello-type towers of concrete that had been left after the War. In those days, we could 'travel' almost all the way between Barkingside and Newbury Park Stations without touching the ground for more than a couple of minutes. I cannot recall if we were ever caught by sharp-eyed railway officials, but it was great fun anyway! In later years, some school chums and I took bottles of fizzy Tizer and an Oxo tin of jam sandwiches up to the aerodrome for impromptu picnics.

Saturdays were very special for all Village children. This was when we received our pocket money, and the amount allocated was fixed, according to age, by the omnipotent Office. It was, however, only handed out to those who had behaved themselves during the week. Deductions were made for bad behaviour, and there were *no* payouts in the event of acts of downright insubordination. Sugar had come 'off ration' after the War. In 1956, however, sweet rationing was re-introduced for a short period. I remember going to the local newsagents opposite the Village in the company of our bossy big girls. We had all been issued with ration books. I was probably given 'thruppence' to spend on sweets – not much in today's money but a great deal could be purchased in those days for that amount. Monkey nuts were favourite of mine, as were sherbet dabs and 'Palm' toffee (banana flavour); and how about "Two ounces of bon-bons, please"?

As soon as we left the shop, the big girls descended upon us little ones, trying to separate us from our sweeties, the beasts! Then one of my friends came up with a solution which actually worked, for a short time anyway. Us 'little uns' were urged to chew up our sweets and spit them back into the bags whilst the older girls were choosing their sweets in the shop!

People outside the Villages used to feel sorry for Barnardo children sometimes, when they weren't looking down their noses at us. Some of us *did* have an unhappy time there, but one could say that of children who lived with their own families.

In those days, the seasons were clearly defined: spring, summer, autumn and winter. The following, although these seasons have been placed intentionally out of order, should more than adequately prove to the reader that…

THERE *WERE* SOME HAPPY TIMES!

SUMMER

I can remember some happy times;
Cloudless skies of blue.
Baggy swimsuit,
Candyfloss,
Lots of things to do!
We had many hours of fun
Walking on the 'prom';
Long brown legs
And sticks of rock.
Sails with 'Uncle Tom'!
Hear the music playing loud
On the sunny pier!
Scenic railway,
Ghost train –
Shrieks of joy, *and* fear!
Sports day! Navy knickers, Aertex shirt,
Running, oh so fast!
Silver medals,
Grins of pride;
'First' mostly, *never* 'last'!

SPRING

Standing on the toilet seat,
I can just make out
Cherry blossom on the trees;
Spring is all about!
I feel the softness of their fur;
Kittens, rabbits and
New, exciting
Baby hamsters
Nestling in my hands!
I smooth the folds of my new frock
And love my knitted 'cardie';
Crépe-soled sandals,
Socks of white;
But hurry! Don't be tardy!
Church bells ringing sweetly,
Altar decked with flowers;
Easter eggs and
Simnel cake.
Sudden April showers!

AUTUMN

I wave to playmates in the street;
September – back to school!
Lengths of seaweed
'Tell' the weather;
But autumn's here, it's cool!
I itch in uniform of serge,
Brown with blouse of cream.
'Standard' raincoat
With a hood.
(Fur coats were just a dream!)
Wellingtons of shiny black

Kicking up the leaves.
Crimson sunsets,
Country walks;
And golden corn in sheaves!
I "Oooh!" and "Aaa!" at rockets
On a Guy Fawkes Night;
Hot potatoes,
Chestnuts,
Songs by firelight!

WINTER
I blow out clouds of frosty breath;
Wintertime is here!
Woolly vests and
Long socks;
Jack Frost nips my ear!
Streetlamps peering through the gloom;
Cars can't be seen for fog.
(We townies call it "pea soup";
The weatherman says "smog!")
"I 'it yer first!" – the snowballs fly.
Ice-skating in the park.
Freezing mornings,
Icicles;
Breakfast in the dark!
Christmas trees, books, paints and toys;
Charles Dickens' book *The Chimes*.
Pulling crackers;
Parties.
Yes! There *were* some happy times!

CHAPTER FIVE:
Life In 'My' Cottages

Abide with me, fast falls the eventide;
The darkness deepens…
HENRY FRANCIS LYTE (1793–1847)

PART I: HOME SWEET HOME?

Over the years, numerous people have asked me the question: "What *was* it like in the Village?" Instead of replying, I counter with "What was it like in *your* home?" Their replies, not unnaturally, have been extremely varied:

"I had a loving childhood as an only child."

"Rotten! Mum and dad never really got on, or had any time for us kids."

"There were a lot of us, but our parents didn't have any favourites."

"Mum was a war widow, but she was so good to us we never felt the need of a father." And so on…

Reader, this is exactly how it was for us children in Dr Barnardo's. The lucky children had sympathetic and loving cottage matrons. (Young married couples appeared during the middle fifties.) These youngsters were treated fairly and, as they grew older, were looked up to by the smaller 'fry'.

That I ended up as one of the *un*lucky ones occurred due to a significant event which took place in the Coronation year, 1953. No one, not even the two matrons, could have foreseen at the time just how much their lives and mine would be affected. That 'event' will be dealt with in the final part of this chapter.

During my time in Dr Barnardo's, I lived in four cottages: Burwell Park, Heartsease and Clement, which were in the Village; and Tudor, which was situated in a road that overlooked the Village play area and swimming pool. The most notable years of my life were spent in Tudor and Clement. These cottages were 'run' by Miss C and Miss D.

I first went to them when they were living in Heartsease, but for some curious reason, can remember very little of what occurred during this period. This cottage was situated on the Reception Green, as already mentioned.

I do not know why our matrons were moved outside the Village, but have no doubt that it must have been an exciting experience for all concerned!

Because Tudor was a 'double cottage' (actually two semi-detached houses), the two oldest girls had the luxury of their own bedrooms. At first, I was placed in the Big Girls' bedroom. I remember that my bed was behind the door.

Now, before I go any further, I want to get something off my mind. At the time of this move, I was one of the youngest little girls and, yes, various 'dark deeds' went on in the bedrooms, both in Tudor and, later, in Clement.

However, I have no intention of elaborating on them. It must be remembered that older Barnardo children at that time would have been affected, both emotionally and physically, by the recently-ended war. Many of them would have been evacuated; some would have lost one or both of their parents, and I am certain their family histories would have made grim reading. I therefore blame no one for any subsequent 'trauma' that *I* suffered over the years, except to state that I was left with an intense dislike of being touched, affectionately or otherwise, by females.

I recognised this as a true phobia when I grew older, and even today I do not feel comfortable if women try to get 'too close' to me, particularly in confined areas such as crowded buses or changing rooms. I also get extremely restless if women sit behind me in church.

Strangely enough, this problem was never to trouble me in Greece, where I lived and worked from 1974 to the early eighties. Here, I formed close and lasting relationships with a number of women, *and* their families.

* * *

When we moved to Tudor, we were allowed to keep pets because there was a large double garden and a shed which had been set aside for the purpose of housing them. I think the matrons 'shared' Cuthbert the cat but Timmy and Rosie, the two tortoises, belonged to all of us. They were *my* favourites. Holes had been drilled into their shells (by a vet) and long cords threaded through. They were thus able to roam happily around the gardens.

At one time, we had some hamsters and a rabbit, but I do not think they stayed very long and were certainly given away before we moved back to the Village.

Miss C loved flowers and 'her' garden became a veritable Thing of Beauty, in which she spent most of her leisure hours. There was a rockery too, which separated her garden from the girls' play green, where we built our bonfires on Guy Fawkes Night. The herbaceous borders were dazzling and some of *her* favourite flowers have remained mine to this day: godetias, love-in-a-mist, and most types of poppies, to mention just a few. There was an enormous double-lilac bush which had sweetly scented purple-and-white blossoms in season. A loganberry hedge had been planted by some previous owners, and we youngsters all enjoyed our first taste of this rather exotic fruit.

Miss C's pride and joy, however, were her tomato plants. One day there arose an enormous 'kerfuffle'; the tomatoes had been attacked! At first, it was suspected that a neighbouring cat, or maybe a fox, had sampled them, as they were not yet ripe. Miss C made a closer inspection though, and this proved not to be the case. She decided to do a 'toothbite check' amongst the girls. Only one set of teeth matched the marks on her precious tomatoes, and as this incident occurred not long after *my* two front teeth had been broken (will tell you about this later) I was severely punished!

Fairlop - 8 years old

An additional 'bounty' at Tudor was revealed when a rhubarb plant was discovered to be thriving beneath the large coke pile next to one of the sheds. For some reason, the rhubarb considered this area to be its Shangri-La. Miss C would make mouthwatering 'crumbles' and pies with it.

From time to time, bullying would break out amongst the girls. This sort of thing, of course, occurs whether children live in a 'home' or in an exclusive boarding school. One day I was standing on a small box at the girls' bathroom sink, busily brushing my teeth. I was alone, and totally absorbed in my task. Suddenly, my head was grabbed from behind and slammed down onto the edge of the porcelain sink. The force of the blow almost knocked me out. I remember spitting out blood and bits of tooth as I fell to the floor screaming with pain. The big girl responsible for this attack was always creeping up behind one or the other of us younger girls, and would push, punch or pinch us for no reason whatever, and always when she knew the matrons were not about.

Another particularly nasty act of bullying occurred some time later. There was a quiet, inoffensive older girl called Diane living with us. Diane used to work in the outpatients' department at the Village isolation hospital. Her job was to wheel the basket containing medicines around the Village and deliver them to various cottages. One day, Diane and a girl whom I shall call Janet had an argument, which was almost certainly started by Janet, who was the lively and aggressive type. The row had begun in the garden and Janet ran into our playroom, which had a wood-and-glass-paned door. Then she slammed and locked it. Diane ran after her, assuming that the door was only ajar. Both her hands went straight through the glass panes, and were horribly injured.

'Tale bearing' also occurred, but I think the matrons were usually able to sort out fact from fiction. The severity of any punishments depended upon the disposition of the matron concerned. Miss D was the 'waspish' type, and I once heard her being referred to as "all white and spiteful", so if I misbehaved, I could expect anything from a sharp slapping to "No jam on your bread for a week". The latter was the greater punishment as I had a very sweet tooth. Miss C was more subtle in her methods of discipline, but no less effective. If I remember correctly, it was she who introduced the 'double punishment' which was to cause me increasing misery as I grew older, more aware and less tolerant of injustices. Let me explain her system to the reader.

I have in my possession, both in book and video documentary form, the story of *The Conquest of Devil's Island,* which was written by Major Charles Péan of the French Salvation Army. In his book, Charles Péan mentions the notorious system of 'doublage'. A prisoner would complete his sentence of, say, fifteen years. At the end of this time, another fifteen years would be added onto the original sentence, during which time he was not permitted to leave the island.

This meant that the unfortunate man remained a prisoner: a victim of 'back-to-back' punishment. Very few men survived this iniquitous treatment, particularly if their original sentence had been a long one.

The manner in which Matron C's doublage worked was as follows, and I would mention that it was to be reserved almost exclusively for me during my last few years in her care. I would be punished for a misdemeanour that usually came to her notice via tale telling. Miss C would often be certain either that I was not guilty at all or that the transgression had been a venial one. No matter; punishment followed and consisted of withdrawing a 'privilege' such as going to youth club night, or giving me an extra chore just as I was going out to play. Later on, she would say, "Well, all right; so you weren't in the wrong *that* time, so the punishment will do for the next time, when you *are* guilty!" She would then conveniently 'forget' the initial incident that had resulted in the unearned disciplining, and give me a fresh punishment when I next really *did* wander from the paths of virtue. As the years went on, she was to become less and less discriminating, with the result that I spent most of the time under the scourge of her never-ending doublage.

When I was about eight or nine, an incident occurred which was to result in my becoming a claustrophobic for life. I was being tormented by some of the older girls whilst we were in the garden, and I ran into the house to hide from them. I went upstairs and hid in the large double wardrobe in the big girls' bedroom. The wardrobe was promptly locked by one of the girls, who must have followed me into the house. I remember hearing the click of the lock and immediately tried to get out. In the struggle, the wardrobe fell over and I was doubly trapped. When I was eventually rescued, punishment followed as a matter of course. The fact that I had been trying to escape from bullying was irrelevant.

I am now going to tell you of some of the *good* things that happened in my cottage life, for a change! All of us girls were given a number. This was either sewn into our clothes, together with our name, on Cash's woven name tapes, or marked in with indelible ink. My number was TWO, maybe because my birthday was on the second of the month.

Miss C was a marvellous cook, and whenever she made cakes or puddings, we would get the chance to scrape out the bowl before it was washed. This is where the numbering came into use, and it was rigidly adhered to, at least for the first few years of my life with the matrons.

When the Christmas puddings were being prepared, of course we all had a stir and made a wish. When I was small, my wish was always the same: "Cakes, buns and biscuits… please!" Little gannet!

One Christmas, we were presented with a huge box containing a Hornby-Dublo train set, complete with signal boxes and railway personnel, trees and signs. What a grand time we had when it was all set out on the playroom floor!

Actually, it was so big that it was necessary to fasten back the dividing doors between our playroom and the dining area. Today the train set would almost certainly be classed as a collector's item. I wonder what became of it. We did not have it with us when we moved back into the Village.

Both matrons were efficient bedtime story readers in those pre-television days. Miss C was the best, I think, and she would call us 'little uns' into her bedroom, which was upstairs and next to the big girls' dormitory. Her room was almost always hazy with cigarette smoke, and our eyes would soon start smarting. There would also be occasional throat clearings until we became accustomed to the atmosphere. I cannot recall that we were bothered by this though.

There we would sit, in a semicircle, with our nighties wrapped round our bare toes, and listen spellbound to *Tanglewood Tales* or Hans Christian Andersen's delightful fairy stories. *The Princess and the Pea* was one of my favourites.

Miss D would read to us from *Five Children and It* or the *Ingoldsby Legends*, although I am not sure now that the Legends were really suitable for such an impressionable child as I was growing up to be.

On *very* special occasions, namely when Miss C was in a particularly good mood, we 'listened in' to *Uncle Mac's Children's Hour*. Later on. 'Journ-ee-ee into Space', produced by the euphoniously named Charles Chiltern, sent shivers down at least *one* little spine. I liked 'Lemmy' best, but it was not until many years later that I learnt that he had been played by the exceedingly suave David Jacobs.

I was passionate about reading and at this stage Rudyard Kipling's Mowgli and Kim were my heroes. I used to turn my nightie into a 'dhoti' by dragging the top down to my waist, pulling the long back portion through my skinny brown legs and knotting it in front. I would then jump up and down on my bed and do handstands against the wall, until either a big girl or one of the matrons caught me.

When we first went into Tudor, the two oldest girls were kind to me. They would tuck me up in bed and make it like a cradle. This would be achieved by pulling the sheets and blankets very tightly round the mattress. The resultant 'rocking' effect soon sent me off to sleep. It was the closest I ever came to being hugged.

I was often a very naughty little girlie after 'lights out', and used to try to make the other girls laugh at my antics. This would result in my being hauled out of bed and made to sit on the bottom of the stairs that led to Miss D's room. This was supposed to be a dire punishment and was usually accompanied by either a clump on the ears or a slap on the bottom or the back of the legs. I would then be handed a sheet to hem or a couple of socks to darn, using the good old fashioned wooden 'mushroom'. Matron would say sharply, and with truth, "If you've got so much energy, you might as well make yourself useful!"

There I would sit, in "splendid isolation", contentedly absorbed with my needlework, listening dreamily to Miss D's piano playing. I can date my love for Chopin's *Nocturnes* from this period in my life. Miss

D was an accomplished pianist – an LRAM I think – and gave private lessons. In time I became skilful both at darning and plain sewing.

On one occasion, I was brought down when I had become overwrought during a summer thunderstorm. I had been allowed to bring my teddy bear with me as a 'comforter', so I was obviously not being punished.

Suddenly, there was a terrific clap of thunder, and I clasped teddy tightly to my chest in fright. How it happened I do not know but... his head fell off! I was terrified and threw him down. I have never owned a teddy bear since.

Throughout my stay in Tudor, I was being treated with Luminal, which was at that time the sovereign remedy for both epilepsy and whooping cough. Interestingly, it was also used to treat such diverse complaints as vomiting in pregnancy, pruritus, vertigo and neurosis. It was advertised as being "The drug of a thousand uses"!

It was also in Tudor that I started sleepwalking. I have no idea when it began, but think it might have had something to do with the reason for my being eventually moved out of the big girls' room.

I would get into the children's bath, having dragged a blanket with me. There I would be found, sound asleep, with my head at the tap end! I was never punished for these nightly wanderings. My subsequent liveliness in the little ones' bedroom was almost certainly due to being removed to an environment where I felt safer.

Both in the Cottage and at school, I had to be watched at all times. This was *not* because I was a bad child, but one simply did not know what I would get up to next! I would regularly wander off if visitors came to the Cottage, even if they were familiar ones. Young people today would say "She wanted her own space" and they would, of course, be perfectly right. On one occasion I did not get away in time... with disastrous results!

A lady called 'Aunty Mabel' used to visit us at Tudor. I think she was a musical friend of both matrons. She grabbed hold of me as I was running past her, and put me onto her lap, holding me close to her rather capacious bosom. To this day, I can remember that she smelt of Parma Violets and wore a fussy white blouse. I was *so* scared, that I promptly 'wet' on her! I do not recall my punishment, but I *do* know that apart from the times I was put out for adoption, this was the only occasion on which I disgraced myself in this manner.

To return to my 'wanderings off' as a child, I have to admit that although I am now well past sixty, I still experience the need to distance myself when surrounded by too many people, particularly if females predominate. Old habits do indeed die hard!

The reader will by now have realised that I was rather a mischievous child: "Find that Susan Plumb! She's too quiet; she must be up to *something*!" and I generally was!

Fairlop – 9 years old

I will mention three of the 'somethings' I enjoyed doing when I was younger, although two of them were potentially dangerous, even at that time. During the summer months I could be found happily chipping paint off gates or windowsills; actually I was 'popping' the paint bubbles that had been caused by the heat. I would then lick my fingers and rub them carelessly down the front of my 'pinnie' before going into meals. I was informed years later that in those days, green paint generally contained a trace of arsenic, and other colours most certainly had lead in them.

Another absorbing game on a hot day would be 'ant hilling'. I would collect tiny twigs and stick them into anthills, stir them up and sit back and marvel at the chaos I had caused. On one occasion, however, I made the mistake of trying to prevent the ants exiting their hill... by sitting down on top of it. Unfortunately, these ants were of the red variety, and I became an intensely painful exemplification of the phrase "She must have ants in her pants"!

In those early post-war days, there was a great deal of work going on in repairing war damage and constructing temporary accommodation for people who had lost their homes. One of the materials used was asbestos. For my younger readers, I give here a description of this substance, taken from *Pears Cyclopaedia* of 1943:

"Asbestos designates a peculiar form of mineral occurring in crystals in pyroxene, and massed together. It is fireproof. Found in Cornwall and some parts of Scotland, but the finest comes from Savoy and it is also abundant in Canada and Tasmania.

Because there were no skips for builders' waste at that time, rubbish would be dumped haphazardly either in the road adjacent to the workplace or, more often than not, in lanes and alleyways at the backs of houses. At the bottom of our back garden at Tudor there was an alleyway that ran the full length of the street we lived on. I often used to rummage through the piles of rubbish that were dumped here, in the hope of finding offcuts of asbestos. I would then get a piece of broken brick or slate and scrape away until I had reduced my 'find' to a handful of soft, white powder. What fun! Throw it up into the air and watch it float gently to the ground as 'real' snow! If I was caught doing this (and I think it only happened twice), woe betide! A scrubbing with carbolic soap and a slapping, or was it bed with no tea, *and* the slapping?!

I should never have been punished at all, since I was far too young to know the dangers of this particular 'play'. It was to be years before the dark shadow of mesothelioma became substance, and the public became bitterly aware of the dangers of this widely-used building material. Thank goodness asbestos had been phased out, or I would be forced here to tell youngsters *not* to "try this at home"!

For all my naughtiness, I appear to have been born with a natural integrity. On one noteworthy occasion, I found a purse in the street when I was with a group of Village children. We were going to play in the local recreation ground opposite the Village, on the Cranbrook Road side. The purse was heavy, so I knew there was money in it. One of the children tried to tempt me to share it out, but instead, I ran to the local police station nearby. My head did not reach the top of the desk as I handed the purse over to the duty sergeant and gave him my details.

Barkingside Police Station

A few days later, a small parcel arrived at the Cottage, addressed to me. It contained some sweets and five shillings – an immense sum in those days. There was a note attached which read – and I can recall the exact words today – "To Susan, an honest little girl, with my best wishes, H. Ranger".

Oh, I forgot to tell you. I *did* steal once, but nobody tempted me; I did it all on my own! It happened thus. During the winter months all us girls in Tudor were given large spoonfuls of malt extract once a week. I loved this *so* much and looked forward to my weekly dose with such longing that one day I just could not wait for 'malt night' to come round. I crept into the large pantry and lifted the heavy jar down from its shelf; but where could I hide it until bedtime?

Being a very agile little girl, however, I solved this problem by clambering onto the headrail of my bed, which was placed next to the communal wardrobe, and carefully placed the malt out of sight. The matrons must have 'cottoned on' immediately, because malt night was brought forward and a thorough search made of all the bedrooms. I remember *that* punishment well: no malt, but an extra-long dose of syrup of figs. Eeugh!

In those far-off days, winters could be very tough indeed, with ice patterns forming on the *inside* of our windows. Small children were clad in lovely woollen three-piece outfits of coat, leggings, and bonnet or hat which usually had earflaps. Then for some stupid, unknown reason an order must have been issued by Head Office in Stepney that these suits were to be discontinued. The unhappy result of this was that almost all of us small children became plagued by 'chaps'. These were blister-like rashes and they would itch so much that we scratched ourselves raw on the backs and insides of our legs. Oh, how painful they were!

I can vividly recall sobbing whilst my poor little legs were being vigorously rubbed with, I think, petroleum jelly. Our scrawny chests were then rubbed and massaged with camphorated oil – later on, 'Vick' – because the wearing of liberty bodices had also been considered unnecessary.

These bodices were in fact cosy little waistcoats made of flannel, and were worn under our vests. I think I also wore mine at night, because I enjoyed chewing the rubber buttons under the bedclothes. In time, the buttons became so chewed up that the bodice could not be fastened properly.

I really *must* have been an odd child, because apart from my 'wanderings off', I had one or two other curious habits. One of these involved breaking the teeth off combs and inserting them into the tiny bottles which were to be found in my toy sweet shop. I also used to like collecting the coloured chips of marble which I found on the graves in Barkingside Cemetery. I would do this during Sunday afternoon walks. The chips would then be put into old matchboxes and hidden round the garden; my treasure trove!

To this day, my bathroom shelves and large workbox-on-wheels are crammed with small bottles and boxes containing a miscellany of tiny objects such as odd beads, scraps of ribbon and bits of broken jewellery which "might come in useful one day"!

I cannot recall that I cried much as a child, but I was definitely a sulker. When I was sent to bed with no tea, I would put my head under the bedclothes and talk to myself. I wonder what I said!

At the beginning of my story, I mentioned poor 'Topsy'. She and I had something else in common besides having been rejected at birth: we were habitual face-pullers. and could put a world of meaning into a facial contortion! Whenever I was told off for some peccadillo, I would rarely talk back. Instead, I would stand straight and roll my eyes upwards or cross them, just like Topsy. My lips would become pursed up "like a Ubangi" as the matrons would say (Whatever was *that*? I wondered) and I would scowl menacingly. It became very difficult for the matrons or teachers to tell if I had been guilty of a particular naughtiness unless I was actually caught in the act.

I did not tell tales, but would stand my ground, repeating, "I didn't do it! I didn't do it!" Needless to say, this usually fell upon deaf ears.

Even at that early stage in my life, I was a child of passion. One day,

I had been invited to tea at a school chum's house; I was in Fairlop Juniors at the time. As my friend's mother and I were returning to Tudor, along Tanners Lane, I made a remark in which I used the phrase "I *hate*…!" with great intensity. Mrs 'T' stopped short and read me a severe lecture about "…little girls using such a strong word, especially when you don't really understand it!" I wonder what it was I had "hated" so much.

Although I was a tomboy and revelled in playing boys' games, I had very little to do with men, although our doctor at the Village hospital and the Colonel were important in my young life. When young couples took charge of cottages, I can remember wishing I could be in one of their homes, with a *real* dad. When I went to outside school there were, of course, male teachers, and Sunday school instructors, whom we shall encounter later on.

There were also Miss C's two brothers, which leads me neatly into a description of the matrons.

PART II: THE MATRONS

Although I have no idea who was the older of the two matrons, I am going to commence with Miss D. The reason for this is that as I write, my hand is shaking and my heartbeat has increased considerably. I want to get this over and done with as soon as possible, so that I can move on. I cannot recall a time when I ever felt at ease with Miss D. My child's instinct made it abundantly clear that she did not like me. I was never to know the reason for this, but it is of significance, I think, to mention that this dislike was apparent *before* the advent of the 'sisters', whom we shall meet later. This aversion towards me became more active as I grew older.

CLACTON – L-R 'Miss D', Susan, 'Miss C''

Miss D was below average height, bespectacled, nimble and always well dressed. I can see her now, in her crackly starched (later nylon) overalls of primrose yellow or light blue. On her feet she usually wore tan Cuban-heeled shoes which tap-tapped bossily along the passages so loudly that we girls could pinpoint her whereabouts in the Cottage most of the time. I say *most* of the time, because if she had cause to suspect one of us – usually *me*! – of being up to something, she was quite able to creep up behind us without a sound.

In those early years at Tudor, we girls would cluster round her piano and sing songs and hymns, or practice Sunday school choruses. I loved these times, but they gradually petered out.

Miss D had a particularly unpleasant habit of never wasting food. She would clutter up the big gas refrigerator with saucers and/or egg cups containing, say, two peas, half a carrot and a couple of stewed prunes. On Miss C's days off, these oddments would be tipped into a pie dish or saucepan, sketchily cooked and served up to us long-suffering girls at mealtimes. This habit of hers was extremely annoying to Miss C, and I think they often 'had words' about it.

Miss D had one sister whom she greatly resembled. Matrons' relatives were generally called Aunty or Uncle, and some of them were very kind to the children. Miss D was a nature lover and would never let any of us girls harm insects. She would double check all open crockery and containers before they were used, to ensure that there were "no little creatures inside".

In retrospect, I find this mania of hers for kindness to 'little things' oddly at variance with her frequent acts of spite towards children she did not like. Her voice was as brisk as her movements – clear and sharp. If she had it in for you, your only solution was to keep her at a distance – not an easy thing to do in a crowded cottage, believe me!

I think my feelings towards her were a mixture of frustration and deepening hostility. The frustration I experienced was due to the fact that although she had once hinted at the possibility of giving me piano lessons, she conveniently forgot about them when the sisters arrived. My developing enthusiasm for music and singing was thus brought to an abrupt end, and I know that I never forgave her for this.

The deepening hostility was caused by my inability to ever do anything right in her eyes. It was Miss D, I am certain, who coined the phrase 'Notice Me!' It became my handle when I was about eight years old and remained so until I left the Village. It was used by both matrons – always in a derogatory fashion. And that's enough about Miss D, for the time being!

Miss C was tall and spare, with large hands and feet. She had crinkly hair, which was always confined in a net, and had the slight stoop that most tall people have. Although there was nothing masculine about her, I persisted in looking upon her as being essentially male. This was probably because she moved around the Cottage in a permanent haze of pungent tobacco smoke! An untipped John Players Senior Service was always clamped between her tobacco-stained teeth. Her chain-smoking habit was almost certainly responsible for some of my health problems: breathlessness; sore eyes; and frequent visits to the isolation hospital, suffering from abscesses in one or both ears.

I also had a short, dry cough, but this could also have been due to a nervous habit, although the matrons would never have admitted that such a thing was possible!

In spite of the fact that Miss C was almost as strict as Miss D, she was not unduly vindictive, and I gravitated towards her at a very early stage in my life with her. She used to wear two beautiful bangles on her upper arms. One was of soft gold, through which she used to thread her handkerchief – not very hygienic! The other bangle was a lovely ivory one, which I always wished were mine.

I have already mentioned Miss C's culinary skills, and can almost smell the delicious aroma of her rabbit pie or stew as I write! These were very economical and highly nutritious meals in those pre-myxamatosis days. She also had what people called a 'pastry hand'. Although Miss C's cooking was excellent and I was not a fussy eater, I *detested* greens of any kind. In those early years, salads (in our cottage at any rate!) were eaten without the 'refinement' of Heinz salad cream, although Branston's piccalilli appeared at the table. Neither were 'meat and two veg' dinners accompanied by today's seemingly obligatory array of sauces to add piquancy to their flavour. I would also like to mention here that chips never appeared on our menu: probably considered "too common"!

There were two ways of disposing of the hated cabbage or lettuce. I would either slip the cabbage into my 'pinnie' pocket, using a sleight of hand quite remarkable in one so young, or I would carefully arrange the lettuce leaves in a circle underneath my plate, hoping that they would drop discreetly onto the floor when our plates were collected.

I needn't have bothered. Both methods were almost immediately observed by one or the other of the matrons, but they would wait until plate collecting had taken place before they 'struck'. The abhorrent comestible would then be retrieved, placed onto my plate, and I would be forced to eat it. There I would sit, head bowed, the tears dripping down my nose and mingling sadly with the green juice dribbling from my protesting mouth as I laboriously chewed and swallowed under the eagle eye of the matrons. Needless to say, I generally received a box on the ears to facilitate my progress!

Eventually, a permanent solution to this problem was found. It was decreed that I should be served with the green stuff first... "and *then* she can have the rest of her dinner". It was an unpalatable but excellent lesson in not wasting food that was "good for me"!

Miss C's habit of smoking whilst cooking also posed problems. However, we girls became accustomed to philosophically blowing any ash residue off plates of food before they were taken into the dining room.

Miss C had two brothers and a sister, whom I *was* allowed to call Aunty and Uncle. They were as tall as she was, and I became very fond of them. Both sisters were expert knitters, as indeed were many women at that 'make do and mend' period, both during and after the War. In those days, practically everything apart from formal mens' suits and rainwear could be knitted. I was an apt pupil and learnt, at a surprisingly young age, that the two most important lessons to memorise are 'tension' and 'finish'. To this day, I still knit most of my jumpers, socks and even warm winter underwear.

The theatre and stage were Miss C's passions. I remember once going with her to see *Swan Lake*, but I did not enjoy it. I thought it then, as indeed now, a waste of good music to have to sit and watch grown-ups prancing around on a stage. She was an avid reader; John Dickson Carr, Ngaio Marsh and Eric Ambler being among her favourite authors. I think it was Miss C who let me have first grabs at the boxes of books that used to arrive at the Cottage, although exactly where they came from I was never to discover.

My greatest regret is that I was never able to fully develop what could have been an emotionally stabilising rapport with her.

PART III: THE SISTERS

The time has now arrived for me to tell you about the significant event referred to in Part I of this chapter. As I start to write about this period, which was to have such a far-reaching and damaging effect upon my life long after I left the Village, I become once more subject to an attack of 'nerves'. However, it began, as indeed these calamitous events in our lives so often do, perfectly innocuously.

Well, here goes! I am going to put the whole thing into rhyme; this will make it somewhat easier for me later.

THE SISTERS
I remember, oh so very well,
The day they came.
We gathered round
And stared at them – the sisters!

I remember their pale, baby faces;
Matching frocks of blue (far too long),
With polka dots of white – the sisters!

I remember the matrons' expressions
As they picked them up, one each,
And held them close.
I looked on, and envied – the sisters!

I remember from that day
They were cosseted and cuddled;
Given toys and precedence
Over us. Who *always* came first? – the sisters!

I remember, oh so well!
Those painful years,
When I yearned for love.
But no; it was only given to – the sisters!

I remember the many gifts;
The weekend treats
With 'aunties', whilst I stayed behind,
Bitterly envious of – the sisters!

They hurt me, even now,
Those pangs of jealousy.
They had *everything*.
I grew lonelier and naughtier
And hated more and more – those sisters!

In a 'normal' family, the arrival of a little brother or sister can be problematical, even if the parents have carefully prepared the older child or children for the event.

The excitement soon wears off. Resentment and jealousy can take over, as baby takes up most of the parents' attention. This can become more marked if there are several years between the births of the first and second child.

In a large family, matters can become complex, as the older children have to move up the ladder to make room for the new arrival.

However, if there is plenty of love to go round, an addition to the family is a wonderfully rewarding experience for all concerned.

In a cottage, where few of the children are related, and are being cared for by unrelated females, as in my case, the situation is very different. I have already mentioned that many Barnardo children had loving and sympathetic cottage guardians; but, as this is very much *my* story, I am only going to relate how *I* was affected by the arrival of the sisters… And how *I* dealt with it all.

There were, of course, incidences in other cottages in the Village where the addition of a very young child was greeted with much pleasure by all the children. I can recall several occasions when, along with other chums, I careered round the Village footpaths, behind one of the older children who was running along, pushing the latest 'baby' in his or her somewhat outmoded pushchair. The child would be made a plaything of, fussed over and included in almost all the games, especially the universally loved 'mothers and fathers'!

The youngster would thus be able to continue to develop as an integral member of the family.

On looking back to the day of the little girls' arrival, I believe that all the warning lights snapped on immediately. Somehow I knew that my life would never be the same again, and nor was it.

The children were not especially attractive, but the matrons were utterly fascinated by them. Miss C chose Sylvia, the younger of the two; and Sheila was snapped up by Miss D. At first, their appearance in the Cottage did not affect me too much; I thought they were a novelty and enjoyed playing with them. It gave me pleasure to walk beside their pushchairs when we all went to the park or on various outings.

The girls had a mother, who visited them regularly. I looked forward to her visits, because she brought bags of sweeties and was very generous with them! She was always accompanied by a female friend. It never occurred to me to wonder why she did not resent her little girls being gradually taken over by the matrons. Maybe she was just glad to see them being treated so well.

My troubles really began when the older girls left the Cottage, and *I* became the Big Girl. This was close to the time when we were about to be moved back into the Village. I was too young, though, to understand the reason for this move, but it was to have a major effect on the matrons.

Miss C was particularly affected, as she lost the beautiful garden she had put so much love into over the years. I was to learn just how devastating this must have been for her over forty years later, when the same thing happened to me. Neither of us had any say on either occasion, and our loss was occasioned by an arbitrary decision made by people who were in a position to control our lives. Our feelings of bitterness and deep resentment must have been very similar.

The cottage we were moved to was called Clement. It was situated next to Cairns House and Clock Tower, which, as the reader already knows, was the home of the formidable Miss G.

The only 'garden' was a weed-choked strip of soil, which was at the side of the Cottage, under the children's bathroom window. Miss C, quite rightly, disdained to have anything to do with it, and it was turned over to our two tortoises and Cuthbert the cat!

Before I continue with my account of how the advent of the sisters affected my life, I think it might be a good idea to give the reader a brief description of what our cottage in the Village looked like. Downstairs, it consisted of a matrons' sitting room and children's playroom, which were situated to the left and right of the front door. A draughty but ornately-tiled passageway divided the Cottage down the middle, although it had a door halfway down it which, however, was usually kept open. There was a large dining room, with a serving hatch into one of the two kitchens. This housed the gas refrigerator and boiler.

Clement Cottage, 1961

Across the corridor was the main kitchen, with its old-fashioned gas stove and kitchen sink with wooden draining board. Opposite the dining room was the cupboard under the stairs, which held all the cleaning paraphernalia and the cleaning woman's overalls.

Next to this was the children's bathroom. It was rather austerely furnished. (In our cottage there were no attractive pictures or decorations; it was purely functional.) There was a large bath, two handbasins and a large porcelain 'laundry' sink. Babies were sometimes bathed in it.

A separate larder, a cloakroom and double toilet for the use of the children completed the downstairs of the Cottage.

Upstairs were two large front dormitories. The matrons' bedrooms were behind these and the four rooms led onto the landing. At the back of the upper floor were the matrons' bathroom (supposed to be strictly off-limits to *all* children) and two smaller bedrooms, one of which was usually occupied by a young 'assistant' matron, who was in training.

The other bedroom, across a small passage, *should* have been occupied by the current Big Girl, and this was to form the root of all my future problems.

By the time we were moved back into the Village, the sisters reigned supreme, although they condescended to play with the other children occasionally.

Many long-term problems had already been caused by the matrons' virtual adoption of these two girls. In retrospect, I feel sorry for them. To use a rather outdated but appropriate phrase, they were being "brought up above their station in life".

From the outset, they had been indulged and taught to believe that they were superior to the other girls in the Cottage. The reason *I* suffered the most was because I had been with the matrons the longest. I had assumed, and not unnaturally since the system prevailed in the other cottages, that I would take over as the important Big Girl. I would be allotted my very own bedroom, which also carried with it an increasing sense of responsibility towards the 'little uns'. Had this longed-for event taken place, my confidence would have received an immense boost and I could have held my head high amongst my peers in the Village.

However, it was not to be. As soon as we moved into Clement, the sisters were given their own room – the one I should have had. My Big Girl's 'rights' had been usurped, and I was forced to occupy one of the dormitories, one of which (mine) had four beds in it. The other room had four beds and a cot, as I recall. The sisters were also the only ones allowed to use the matrons' bathroom, and this was strictly against Village rules.

I grew increasingly resentful at this blatantly unfair treatment. I was also being looked down on by the younger girls, who of course took their example from the sisters. I was picked on constantly. Tales, true or otherwise, were carried to their respective matrons by the sisters, and I became more and more unhappy.

This 'discrimination' gradually became common knowledge in the Village. Some cottage heads went to Miss G and requested that I be 'removed to safety' in their own cottages, but nothing ever came of it. Maybe Miss G thought the matter was of no importance, or the matrons had become so accustomed to their 'whipping boy' that they were not at all anxious to let her go!

Times were changing and it was becoming more difficult to be (at least openly) cruel to the children with impunity. This change came too late to be of any real benefit to me though.

Over the years I had become exceedingly submissive to various forms of unkindness, and took this ill treatment as my due. As I grew older, however, I *did* try to fight back, using the only weapons at my disposal: sulkiness, cold silence and, when sorely tried, insolence. Needless to say, these were all punishable offences!

One of the new married couples in the Village became especially fond of me, and I used to visit their cottage regularly. Mr 'K' instructed us boys and girls on the sports field. This couple persisted in their requests to have me moved to their cottage, but they were just as persistently turned down. If I had gone to this couple, my life would have been very, very different.

I only found out about all this some years after I left Barnardo's. By then it was, of course, too late.

As I grew older, my presence at the dining room table became intolerable to the sisters. They always sat at the head and tail of the table, next to their own particular matron, whom by this time they were permitted to address in terms of great affection.

I was therefore relegated to a chair at the small table by the serving hatch. This was in a cramped area just behind the dining room door. This table held the large metal teapot and milk jug. It was also crowded with dirty crockery. There I would sit, nose to knees, eating my meals with what appetite I could muster, because by this time I had started to lose interest in my food.

Should any of the children have occasion to approach the table, they would call me names such as 'greedy' and 'pig' and/or 'accidentally' jog my elbow so I spilled my food or drink. If one of the matrons happened to be standing at the serving table, I would often either be prodded painfully in the back or 'biffed' across the head, which was usually buried in one of my school books. This treatment continued until I left the Village.

The fact that the sisters became so insufferable was due entirely to the 'exclusive' upbringing they received from the matrons.

They were, after all, only 'Barnardo kids' like the rest of us, and should have been treated accordingly.

CHAPTER SIX:
Education

Father, lead me day by day
Ever in Thine own good way;
Teach me to be pure and true,
Show me what I ought to do.

... ...

When I'm tempted to do wrong,
Make me steadfast, wise and strong;
And, when all alone I stand,
Shield me with Thy mighty hand.
JOHN PAGE HOPPS (1834–1911)

PART I: PRIMARY AND JUNIOR SCHOOLS

When I came into possession of my Barnardo's file, I noticed that the only *complete* set of records that existed was my school reports. These commenced in 1950 with a summer term report from Mossford Primary School, and ended with the final secondary school report dated the 21st of July 1961.

I have read these reports over and over again. Each time I do so, I experience feelings of intense sadness at the waste of so much of what one teacher used to call my "executive ability".

I left the Village infants school, called Mossford, in 1952 and the last sentence written in that report, by Miss 'U', the headmistress, makes disturbing reading:

She does not mix much with the other children and does not seem to be very happy.

It was only in January of this year that I came to understand fully the sequence of events that led to this observation having been made by Miss U, though she would almost certainly not have been enlightened at the time.

From Mossford School, I was sent out to Fairlop Infants. I was to remain at Fairlop until 1961. In spite of the worrying final report from Mossford, I made a good start at my new school.

At the infants school, I gained top marks in all subjects except 'number', which was how arithmetic was described at that time. The teacher's comments of "Doesn't like it and does not try much" and "Very careless" were to echo and re-echo throughout my entire school career, ending with the "Unteachable!" from my last maths teacher, who was driven to total frustration by my inability and, I must add with truth, unwillingness, to master this subject. To this day, I can still be reduced to tears when trying to count the stitches in a complicated knitting pattern.

I have three vivid memories of those early days. In the first, I am standing in a large room with a crowd of other children. We are being shepherded along in front of some low trestle tables, upon which have been placed a seemingly endless array of cards. All these cards are covered in a brightly coloured polka-dot pattern. A teacher comes up to me and tells me I must "try and see if you can find a number in each pretty card" The memory begins to fade as I lean over and squint down at a card. I can only assume, now, that we are all being given a rudimentary 'sight test'!

The second memory finds me standing on the large school sports green. Something quite out of the ordinary is taking place. Is it a circus? Is it a carnival? I am not sure. All I know is that there are hundreds of people milling round. Some are dressed in fantastic costumes. There is, I think, at least one large marquee, and… is that a *donkey* over there? Of one thing I am absolutely certain, and that is the song that is being sung. I can hear it today as I write:

> The sun is a-shining to welcome the day;
> Hey ho! Come to the fair!
> The folk are all singing,
> So happy and gay;
> Hey ho! Come to the fair!

This jolly song was written by Easthope Martin, although, of course, I did not know it then.

There are distractions everywhere, but I was too young and shy to take it all in. However, I believe there were also roundabouts and sideshows. This might have been the once-famous Fairlop Fair; but why was it being held on the school field, or has my memory played tricks with me again, and placed an event in the wrong location? It doesn't really matter: this is, after all, only a *scrapbook* of memories!

My third recollection is of the huge red-and-green steamroller that was situated on the infants' playground.

Nowadays, of course, this would never be allowed, but we had great fun clambering all over this marvellous giant 'toy'. I am sure there must have been one or two accidents on it, because at first it was fenced off, and then it disappeared altogether. Spoilsports!

Before I continue, I should mention that Fairlop school was some distance from the Village. Catching a bus to school was never an option in those days, so all us children used 'Shanks's pony'.

I remember the eerie feeling I experienced as we stood just outside the Village gates in Ley Street. We were waiting to cross the road on a foggy day. These fogs were not called 'pea soupers' for nothing! It was almost impossible to "see your hand in front of your face" because of their extreme density.

The fog was a thick, smokey yellow-grey, and caused many health problems, such as acute bronchitis and rhinitis. Asthmatics, not unnaturally, were also seriously affected.

Loud noises could be dangerously muted, and buses and cars were apt to appear 'out of nowhere', grinding to a halt just a few feet short of a pedestrian, who might have managed to stumble halfway across the road. *If* he was lucky, he would make it safely to the other side, but fatalities were not uncommon. We would then make our way up Craven Gardens.

Once there was a national bus strike, which paralysed London. This proved to be a splendid opportunity for us children to hitch lifts to school on all sorts of unlikely vehicles. I can recall arriving outside the school gates on a milk float once; and on a *very* exciting occasion, some of us were picked up by the local coalman with his horse and cart!

If we happened to take the alternative route to school, we would go down Barkingside High Street. This was a very staid place in those far-off days. I remember Odell's the opticians. There were quite a number of shoe shops (Bata? Freeman, Hardy & Willis?) and a large Co-op furniture store near the post office.

The places I liked the best were Marments the toy shop and the deservedly famous Rossi's ice cream parlour, both of which were situated near Boots the chemist.

On one memorable occasion, I had a lime-flavoured ice cream soda. This was quite expensive at 1s. 9d, but I cannot remember who bought it for me. Until I went to Rome many years later, I was not to taste anything so cool and delicious!

The High Street eventually led to my favourite place: the trolley bus terminal at the junction with Craven Gardens. In the centre of this junction was a huge dip in the ground, which was overgrown with weeds. All the children enjoyed running up and down it, although we often got shouted at by the grown-ups. The dip was actually the remains of a huge World War II bomb crater.

Trolley Terminal Bus

How I loved those mighty trolley buses! Sometimes, whilst they were travelling along the road, one of the 'antennae' would slip off its cable with a flash and crackle. This would force the driver to stop and, studiously ignoring any inconvenience to the vehicles following in his wake, he would hop nimbly out of his seat. Using a long pole, he would 'reactivate' his bus. I used to stand and watch, fascinated, as he hooked the antenna back into place.

I had a hero at this terminal. He was the trolley bus inspector. Clad in his very smart black uniform and 'posh' peaked cap, he ruled supreme – sort of a main attraction. I made a point of always running up to him, though I was probably rather a hindrance as I used to jump about excitedly and chatter all the time. Looking back at this period in my life, I realise that he represented one of my first 'father figures'.

My final school journey memory is of our 'sweet lady' in Fencepiece Road. I think she must have been disabled, because she was always sitting in a chair at her sitting room window. As we passed her house, she would call out and beckon us into her tiny garden. In we would troop and, all talking at once, hold out our greedy little hands for toffees and boiled sweets. She must have been quite a lonely old lady and I for one, grew very fond of her. Upon mature reflection, I wonder if this fondness was due to the fact that here was at least *one* female who didn't want to boss me about and who would certainly not have been able to catch me if I made a run for it! Of course, though, it could just have been good old 'cupboard love'!

One of the first things Village children learnt when they moved to 'outside school' was that Barnardo children, regardless of their colour, were not liked very much, either by schools in general or the locals in particular. I have spoken to several Old Boys and Girls about this subject, and we all agreed that there *was* an enormous stigma attached to being an inmate of the Village.

"Them Barnardo kids must've done it!" was a phrase that persisted throughout our school years. When any acts of damage to school or public property occurred, or if a theft was reported, Barnardo children would be hauled up before the powers-that-be and given a sound grilling. In fact, it was comparatively rare for any of us to do anything really bad as punishments that followed were severe, both at school *and* in our cottages!

These were the good old days I have mentioned before, when corporal punishment was the norm. The cane was used even in the girls' secondary school, and I can recall several painful incidences of being sent to the headmistress for physical chastisement.

During 1955, my eyesight had begun to deteriorate and spectacles were prescribed. Nowadays, children are extremely fortunate as they are able to make their own choice from an endless array of attractive frames. In my day, only one style was available to us and it was *dire*. The frame and portion of the sidearms were constructed out of a plastic type of material and the colour was, I think, a uniform browny-red. The part that actually hooked behind the ears was simply a length of ridiculously flexible wire, and I should imagine that there were very few children who did not, at some time or other, twist these wires out of shape. I know *I* did because I detested wearing the wretched things.

So, in addition to being teased because of my odd surname, I now had to endure nicknames such as Plumbie Four Eyes and Goggle Face. It should therefore come as no surprise to anyone that no photographs exist of me wearing glasses! Whenever school photographs were being taken, I would either tuck them into my gymslip pocket or place my arms carefully over them, as in this photograph taken when I was thirteen.

My junior school years ended at summer term 1956. By this time, I had begun to show real promise: I was first in the class of thirty pupils. Teacher's comment: "This result shows what Susan can do if she puts out her best effort." Even our formidable headmaster has a good word to say for me: "Susan has done well this term and we hope she will do well in the secondary modern school."

Would she though? We shall see!

Fairlop - 13 years old

Events that were taking place in the Cottage had not yet proved too damaging to my scholastic achievements. I left junior school surrounded by an aura of hope. I had even won a prestigious inter-school essay competition. I think it was entitled: From Cocoa Bean to Chocolate Bar.

We had been learning how Cadbury (or was it Fry's?) made their famous chocolate products, and this entailed either a documentary film and/or visit to an actual factory – my memory is rather hazy on the point. However, I do remember the thrill I experienced when teacher read out *my* name as being the overall winner!

I was presented with a certificate and a large box of assorted chocolate goodies. Unfortunately I was not permitted to keep them to myself. As soon as school was over, the boys 'jumped' me, and although I made a spirited dash for it, they chased me all the way down the long Tomswood Hill, eventually catching up and relieving me of my prize!

Before leaving the subject of how I fared at junior school, it might amuse the reader to take a peep at some of the teachers' comments as to my general behaviour. I was a "very talkative girl … Behaviour fair – poor." (1954)

"All Susan's work is spoilt by her inattentiveness in class. Her behaviour in the classroom has deteriorated this term." (summer 1955)

"Susan has improved both in work and behaviour. She is still rather noisy … but in spite of this she never gives in any work which is not her best effort, and while at work is too interested to be distracted." (Christmas term, 1955)

Actually, the last part of the report (commencing with my being rather noisy) is a fair assessment of myself, as I am to this very day!

PART II: SECONDARY SCHOOL

As we have seen, I left junior school in an aura of hope. When I arrived at the girl's secondary school I think I must have been one of the first coloured Barnardo children to go straight into the 'A' stream. The fact that I remained there was almost certainly due to the concerted efforts of one or two enlightened senior teachers. They recognised my latent potential and had obviously been able to out-manoeuvre the headmistress, whom I am certain would dearly have liked to relegate me to a lower form. In other words, put me 'in my place'!

I would just mention here that at almost all schools in the borough,the only 'children of colour', as we were called then, were from Dr Barnardo's Homes.

Fairlop School

Fairlop Girls' School must have been an attractive place in 1956. There was a small garden in the grounds, which contained a minute rockery and fishpond. The very senior girls and prefects would sit around this pond during playtime and dinner hour, either reading or chatting. I held these almost-adults in great awe and was always being pulled up by them for some misdemeanour, such as running on the stairs or talking in the corridors ("Single file and NO TALKING back there!")

My readers are already well aware that I was extremely mischievous. Throughout my secondary school career, reports bristled with comments such as "Rather uncontrolled", "Needs constant supervision" and "Improved, but still needs watching"!

I was certainly being 'watched' on one hot day during my first term. At that time, the senior boys' athletics area took up about a third of the huge sports field, which ran the full length of the entire school, from

Fencepiece Road to Colvin Gardens.

The boys had a cricket pavilion and a set of enticing bowling 'nets'. I used to be able to climb like a monkey, and on this particular day, was observed scrambling halfway up one side of these nets, for a 'dare', as I recall. After being ordered peremptorily to "get down *immediately!*" or words to that effect, I was sent to the headmistress for punishment. Not a very auspicious start, was it? It must be remembered, too, that these school 'chastisements' were generally 'duplicated' in the Cottage at a later stage!

The senior boys were eventually moved to the Fullwell Cross area. Their brand new school was also used for evening classes later on, and I think I used to attend English literature and shorthand classes.

This school is now called King Solomons.

Morning assemblies in the fifties and early sixties were only attended by girls of the Protestant faith, or no faith at all. Catholic and Jewish girls were allowed to remain in the classrooms, and I for one envied them because they used to sit on the desks and chatter happily until the rest of us trooped back.

There was a great deal of inattentiveness during assembly, and some of the girls would even employ the time by picking bits of fluff off the 'woollies' of the girls in front of them. This fluff would be carefully rolled into balls, and there were 'competitions' to see who could achieve the biggest ball.

Whispering or any overt movement was kept to a minimum, however, as the prefects were sharp-eyed and not above sending culprits to their form mistresses for disciplining. Most of the time such behaviour was considered trivial and we would be let off with, say, fifty lines. "I must not misbehave during assembly" was one I can remember losing my playtime to.

The classrooms held about forty pupils; and teachers, both male and female, were generally very strict.

One of the senior boys told me that his form master had his own method of dealing out punishment to boys who talked or were inattentive during his maths lessons. Mr 'T' would be busy putting up sums on the blackboard, seemingly fully engrossed in his task. Suddenly, he would whirl round and send his piece of chalk flying across the classroom. It would land a stinging blow on the ear of one of the boys, usually the guilty one! He rarely missed, and must have been gifted with sonar, like bats!

When schoolchildren behaved badly in those halcyon days of corporal punishment, parents rarely 'came up the school' to complain. There was no such nonsense as teachers being reprimanded or losing their jobs for 'assaulting' pupils. If we played up we were kept in after school; we lost our playtime; were given lines, as already mentioned, or, for more obvious acts of insubordination, were publicly admonished during assembly. This last could be *very* humiliating. I much preferred a comparatively private caning to being shamed before the whole school.

The canings were carried out by the head teacher and, as with our Village system, were entered in a punishment book. Needless to say, pupils did *not* argue with the teachers, and there was no redress.

This was the era of school milk at playtime. Immensely heavy steel crates were hauled into the classrooms, and 'milk monitors' chosen. They would hand out straws and the bottles of milk, which contained a third of a pint of full-cream milk. During my time at Fairlop there were surprisingly few milk haters in my classes.

We enjoyed a variety of games during playtime and dinner hour. The senior girls would wander among the youngsters, keeping a lordly eye on us, and there was always a teacher on duty.

Groups of girls would become absorbed in the ancient game of 'five stones'. The game of 'jacks' was a novelty that became fashionable at this time too, both in the Village and at school.

Skipping lasses occasionally became entangled in the long ropes, which sometimes extended for the full width of the playground, and on occasion a sprightly young teacher might join in the fun.

From time to time, exciting new playground 'rages' would occur. I remember when 'Scooby-Doo' appeared on the scene. It probably hailed from America – or Hong Kong? We spent entire playtimes twisting the thin, brightly coloured plastic tubes into fantastic shapes, which could then be 'swapped' amongst school chums.

Then the hula hoop craze arrived! I do not know if it was the fault of my flat feet and 'valgus' ankles, but I could never keep my balance long enough to make even a half-twirl with a hoop. *How* I used to envy those girls who could keep as many as three hoops on the go at once! "It's good for your figure!" and "Look at *me!*" they would cry smugly. Both Scooby-Doo and hula hoops have enjoyed a revival in recent years, and give great pleasure to both girls *and* boys now.

I was to experience the same sense of non-balancing frustration when the Twist made its appearance later on in the early sixties. Even today, I have to lean against a friendly wall in order to put on some of my nether garments, or I topple over!

My real forté was physical education, particularly athletics and netball. The only poor report I have for these lessons was, not surprisingly, written by a teacher whom I detested. She was the tall, stringy type and I disliked the way she 'handled' me over the vaulting boxes, or 'horses'. Her July 1957 comment simply reads nastily: "A poor worker!" Another PT teacher said that I had "ability but is *lazy*", and a third wrote: "Susan's dancing needs more control and concentration". Give me a break... please!

At this time, I would mention that whilst teachers were describing me, off the record, as being 'impulsive', the matrons in my cottage insisted that the *correct* description should have been '*re*pulsive'! Very encouraging, I must say!

These are all rather negative comments, bearing in mind that at that time I was one of the fastest runners in the school. I had represented it on a number of occasions at places such as Ilford's Cricklefields sports fields, and Harlow and Basildon 'new' town's athletics grounds. I was also in the netball team. We played against various local schools, and in my tiny diary for 1961 I read "2nd February – played Caterham. WON 16-7!" Caterham was newly-built school in Clayhall. Its uniform at that time was an eye-putting-out bright blue. On the 10th of March we "played Gearies and WON 19–8!" I cannot think *what* happened here as Gearies was one of the 'crack' local netball teams!

Ilford Town Hall used to host a school Dancing Festival, in which all the local schools took part. We Fairlop girls would practice for this event for hours every week, and I can still hear the PT mistress bawling out such instructions as "NO! You turn to the *right*, not the left, stupid girl!" or "That girl's out of step AGAIN!" but not necessarily at me!

The great day would arrive and we would take our places on stage, in front of an immense audience comprised mainly of proud families and friends. Neither of my cottage matrons ever attended such events when I performed. They were not at all interested in watching me "making an exhibition of yourself!" or "showing your bottom and legs!" I mention these particular comments because I always took the 'boy' parts.

When I look back across the years, I think I must have looked quite captivating, especially when we did the cheerful German dances or the brisk Polish mazurkas. I would be clad in short lederhosen and a billowing white shirt. Long, dazzlingly white socks and neat 'pumps' completed this outfit, and were supplied by the school. I do not remember if we won any awards, but we certainly enjoyed ourselves. The bright lights, the loud music and the huge banks of hydrangeas at the front of the stage; what fun it all was!

The lights fade, and I am back in school again. Rats! It's a Domestic Science lesson. Nowadays, children as young as six or seven are allowed to mess around making cakes instead of concentrating on the 'three Rs'. Before we girls were permitted to put so much as a fingernail on a rolling pin or crack an egg into a bowl of flour, we were instructed into the art of Household Management.

It commenced in Needlework Class. We would puncture our fingers and thumbs each week as we made 'housecraft' caps and aprons. The material used was gaily coloured cotton gingham in red, blue, green or yellow. Although most of us disliked the fussy little mitre-shaped caps, we probably looked quite fetching as we took our places in the

Domestic Science room. All our caps and aprons were embroidered with our own designs, some of which were quite intricate.

During our lesson we were taught, amongst the myriad household tasks, how to wash our clothes (together with the rudiments of personal hygiene), how to set tables for various meals, and... wash dishes. We even learnt how to take apart, clean and reassemble a gas stove! Notes on all aspects of 'D.S.' were written up in our exercise books, complete with diagrams. One particular lesson amuses me, even now, although I am not sure if it took place in domestic science class.

We had been studying General 'Waste Disposal' and teacher told us to draw an example of Getting Rid of Waste. Here is my 'contribution':

M	F	M	F

PUBLIC LAVATORIES

Surely the most forward-thinking public convenience of the period, albeit rather naïve!

I think the first actual baking lesson we were given in my class was to make either rock buns or a simple Victoria sandwich. At this period of my life I had virtually no concept of what time meant. Both in the Cottage and at school, I was so regulated that I had no need to look at clocks. I was seventeen before I was given my first watch. So there I was. I had mixed my ingredients with the help of my partner. (We always worked in pairs for some reason.) It was now time to put the mixture in the oven. Suddenly, teacher pounced on me. "Susan Plumb! How long will it take to cook?"

I promptly, and rather smugly, replied, "Fifteen minutes to quarter of an hour, Miss!" I spent the remainder of *that* lesson almost in tears as I struggled to master the art of telling the time!

For one entire term, our geography class was taught by a male teacher from America. He was probably on a teaching experience holiday at the time. Mr 'O' was tall, wore steel spectacles and had a very overbearing manner. Although we were initially fascinated by his 'Yankee' drawl, I do not think he was especially popular, and he took an almost instant dislike to *me*. I sometimes wondered if my colour had anything to do with this dislike.

Mr O once heard me make a derogatory remark about one of the quieter girls in the class. He strode across the room towards me and thundered out, "What a snotty, undemocratic thing to say!" Every head in the classroom flew up. I was petrified. At this ill-starred moment, the door opened and the headmistress looked in. She must have been passing, and heard Mr O shouting.

I cannot remember what followed, though strange to say, it was *not* corporal punishment. Mr O's rather waspish assessment of my abilities for term ending July 1959 was: "Indifferent worker who is easily distracted!" This was often a fair comment; I rarely worked well with teachers I disliked.

One of my favourite lessons was music. From a very early age I could sing like a little robin, and have already described how much I enjoyed singing round the piano in the Cottage.

There were two music mistresses during my time at Fairlop. I once heard a naughty girl call them "Fatty and Skinny". Miss Z was tall and angular. She wore her hair in a bun and was rarely seen out of rather mannish tweed suits and well-cut brogues, no matter what the weather. This lady had a disconcerting habit of sitting on her desk in front of the girls during the lesson. She would casually hitch up her skirt and display long, salmon-coloured 'directoire' style bloomers; but none of the girls dared giggle.

Mrs T was excessively stout and very quick-tempered.

I remember one lesson of Mrs T's, when we were told to illustrate Handel's *Water Music*, which we had just been listening to on the gramophone: 'Musical Appreciation'. I was hopeless at drawing and could only manage a rather rickety barge sailing down a leaden Thames.

We sang all the good old folk songs such as 'Barbara Allen' and

'Drink to Me Only with Thine Eyes'. I enjoyed the jolly tune of 'Marianina', but the lyrics were numbingly feeble:

O'er the ocean flies a merry fay;
Bright her wings are as a cloud of day…

Well, for heaven's sake, what absolute rubbish!

There was also one called 'The Cockle Gatherers', which I think was of Gaelic origin, and had a tongue-twisting chorus:

Laughter of joy birds
Down on the skerry there;
Laughter of joy birds
While I gather cockles there!

This last verse we sang at railroad speed, but… what*ever* were 'joy birds'?!

Humperdinck's *Hansel and Gretel* was a great favourite with all the girls. The lasses who were chosen to sing Gretel's part tap tap tapped their feet and clap clap clapped their hands boisterously as they pertly informed Hansel, "Then you soon will *dance* like me!" However, as there were other actions involved in this operatic masterpiece, it might just as well have been performed during our dancing classes! Maybe it was? Another 'memory lapse' of mine?

My favourite song, however, was Heinrich Heine's poem 'The Lorelei', which had been set to some beautiful music. Many years later, I was to take a great deal of interest in this ill-fated poet's work. Almost all my reports for music lessons were encouraging. They were only marred by the occasional "Theory needs care", "Lacks concentration", and "Needs more confidence".

School Musical Festivals were held then, as indeed they are today, at Ilford Town Hall. Unfortunately, my memory seems to let me down badly as I try to recall what happened at any of them. I *do* remember the ghastly recorder performances though. They were so tediously repetitive.

Human Biology was not taught in our school at that time. The closest my class ever came to learning about the 'birds and bees' was during a Science lesson. Our teacher was a very smartly dressed lady who wore 'butterfly' spectacles. She had a penchant for dealing out stingingly sarcastic put-downs. As we sat on our high chemistry stools with our elbows on the long wooden tables, which were also fitted with the necessary Bunsen burners, she began to initiate us girls into the thrilling world of differences between males and females. Readers will find what follows hard to believe, but I can assure them it was all perfectly true. I can see the blackboard in front of me as I write.

Mrs 'E' is wearing an attractive emerald-green twinset, complete with its traditional string of pearls. She has on a tweed skirt and her feet are clad in a pair of elegant and expensive high heels. As she raises her hand to the blackboard, her bangles jingle fussily. First, she chalks out the shape of a large rooster, side elevation. He sports a plumy tail and wattles. "This is a male hen," she blithely informs us, and then completely confounds the entire class by adding on an odd-looking 'protuberance', which issues from his chest, just under his beak! Keeping a perfectly straight face, Mrs E blandly tells us the correct biological name for this exciting appendage. There are several embarrassed titters and a few covert nudges ("But what's that *for*?" "What does it *do*?") I cannot recall how the remainder of the lesson proceeded.

School dinners were attended by most children in those far-off days. These meals, though much complained of, were well planned and nutritious. I believe they cost about 3s. 9d. per week during my final terms. As with most schools, fish was rarely served, even on Fridays, because too much was wasted. I enjoyed these dinners, and my favourite meals were shepherd's pie and all suet puddings with meat, followed by jam tart and custard and sponge pudding, especially the chocolate one. There was one more pudding that was not very popular, but which I relished, and here is a puzzle for younger readers: What is the *real* name for 'dead flies in whitewash'? I always managed to get 'seconds' of this! Your grandparents will be able to tell you!

Sometimes, after meals and if it was a sunny day, a classmate and I would sit with our backs against the dinner hut. We would chatter away nineteen to the dozen, setting ourselves impossible tasks such as "Count the blades of grass on the sports field – in twenty seconds". As these tasks became more ridiculous, we would go off into a burst of silly laughter.

At one time, a few of us girls formed a group which we called Our Gang – a name probably gleaned from one of the school comics available at that period, perhaps *Girls' Crystal* or *School Friend*. We used to congregate in the cycle shed at the side of the Art hut. Oh, I must tell you something about that Art hut. It contained a 'bust' of a lady, sculpted in a bilious green clay. Apparently our art mistress had used the formidable headmistress as a model, and I used to be extremely embarrassed if I had to sit next to it. Naked females always made me feel very uncomfortable.

To return to Our Gang, I have no precise recollection of the subjects we gossiped about, although boys were almost certainly on the agenda. Nor can I recall any of the escapades we plotted; it was all innocent 'girl talk', punctuated by bursts of giggling.

My favourite friends at that time were Margaret, who lived almost opposite the school gates, and the twins Sally and Gillian, who were two very 'buzzy' Irish girls. All three were good at lessons, and members of the school netball team.

Gillian became a competent actress and once played the lead in a play, Thornton Wilder's *Our Town*. During this play, John Fawcett's lovely hymn 'Blest Be the Tie that Binds' was sung soulfully whilst the wedding scene was being enacted. I was not allowed to go and see the play.

The twins taught me to cycle when I visited their home after school. Theirs was one of the only homes which I was allowed to visit more than once. I used to be quite envious of their pretty mother and the general family closeness.

On one never-to-be-forgotten occasion, Our Gang and a few other girls had a hair-raising experience with… a fire extinguisher!

We had been mucking about in the assembly hall/gym one dinner hour. In an evil moment, we decided to remove the extinguisher from its wall fitting. There we were, brandishing this heavy implement around when, suddenly, it 'exploded'. At first we were all aghast; rooted to the spot with fear. Then we tried frantically to stem the flow of frothy liquid. This proved impossible and, to make matters worse, a large amount of liquid shot into the school piano, the top of which someone had left open.

I think the only reason we were not all caned, or even expelled, was because we were believed when we explained that we had been "practising our dancing and accidentally fell against the extinguisher". And of course, *no one* 'told tales'!

Let us now take a brief look at how my behaviour was progressing.

Term ending December 1957: "Susan is not a very co-operative member of the form, being inclined to think only of herself. She lacks concentration and dislikes conforming to rules obeyed by the rest of the class." Dear oh dear!

July 1959: "I am pleased with the effort she has made to participate fully in school activities but she has still to realise that consistent courtesy to adults is a very necessary quality." No comment!

In summer 1961, my final academic assessment reads: "Susan has developed well this year. She has remarkable linguistic ability and has reached a good level in nearly all subjects." This was truly a noteworthy comment, given the worsening atmosphere in the Cottage. However, I still needed to "show a more adult attitude", "become steadier" in my behaviour, and "have more confidence" in myself.

My grasshopper-like memory now takes a leap onto a very different subject. During our final terms at Fairlop, we girls were allowed to wear what we liked, as long as it conformed to the school colour scheme.

Trousers were, of course, *not* permitted.

This was the era of the 'paper nylon' petticoat, and these were worn under brown-and-white gingham skirts. Sometimes the girls would rinse out these half-slips in a mixture of sugar and water, which made them excessively crackly and often snagged holes in their nylons! Wide plastic belts encircled slim, and not-so-slim (!) waists. The more fashion conscious lasses had 'graduated' to kitten-heeled shoes, but most of us were content to wear ankle socks and casual shoes, with the then fashionable T-straps or buckles.

By the age of fourteen, I was becoming increasingly self-conscious about what some of the nastier girls called my "beer bottle legs". Actually, they were very shapely. However, I would not feel *really* confident about them until, curious to say, the mini-skirt and 'hot pants' arrived during the middle sixties!

There was a brief fashion, I think in 1959, when fluorescent socks became the rage. Sometimes girls would either wear two entirely different coloured socks, or two socks on each foot. The inside one would then be turned over the outside one – very flashy and extremely daring! The teachers saw to it, however, that this was to be a short lived craze.

Televisions were still quite a luxury item. They were all black and white, and not every home could afford one. Gramophones such as the 'Dansette' were popular, and I remember when Helen Shapiro caused a sensation with her debut record 'You Don't Know'. It was a revelation to all us schoolgirls. She was only FOURTEEN: younger then *we* were! She looked the typical schoolgirl too with short, dark hair and a cheeky grin. I am almost certain that in the first picture we saw of her she was wearing ankle socks, just like us!

Oh, how envious we were! Of course, though, we could all sing better than Helen. It was "just luck" that had rocketed her to fame. In the playground, the Wo-oo, Wo-oo, Woos and Ye-ea, Ye-ea, Ye-eas could be heard everywhere.

One of the biggest contemporary schoolgirl heart-throbs was Frankie Vaughan. His dazzling smile and electrifying performance of 'Green Door' set many a schoolgirl's pulse racing. I saw him on the programme called by us youngsters "London Night at the Sunday Palladium". No one ever wore a straw 'boater' so effectively as Our Frankie. "Give me the moonlight, Give me the Gal, and leave the rest, da, da, da, da, to *me!*" Saucy words in those prim days!

Autograph hunting was yet another craze, and this enjoyed a much longer 'innings'.

I still have my two autograph books. The 1957 one has been written in by Our Gang and contains such old chestnuts as:

> Roses are red; Violets are blue.
> Cabbage is green and so are you!
> – Gillian

'Jones Minor' wrote:
> Don't kiss your boyfriend at the garden gate;
> Love is blind but the neighbours aint!

Another chum penned this piece of deathless verse:

> It's hard to part with the one you love;
> It's hard to say 'Goodbye'.
> But it's harder still to find the towel
> With soap suds in your eye!

Finally, here is the enigmatic but vastly popular:

> 2 Y U R 2 Y U B I C U R 2 Y 4 Me!

Let's see if you young readers can work *that* one out!

Before leaving Fairlop, we girls vied with one another for teachers' autographs, and I was one of the only ones to obtain "All Good Wishes" from the redoubtable Mr O – he who had disliked me so much!

I also have the autograph of Annette Mills, although I have no idea how or where I obtained it. Of course, it might have been given to me at a Barnardo children's party. These were often attended by well-known personalities from the world of entertainment, and I can certainly remember a party where Dave King made an appearance.

Annette Mills was a very popular ventriloquist on children's television, with her Muffin the Mule.

The final entry in my 1961 diary reads: "FRIDAY 21st JULY – left school today. Lots of girls cried. Took addresses down."

By this time, the years of misery I had endured in the Cottage had taken their toll of my ability to have faith in myself. It did not seem to matter much to either of the matrons how well I had done in my last term, and life, from now on, was going to be even more of a struggle

I was deeply apprehensive about facing the outside world. Unfortunately, events were to prove that I had very good reason for my fears.

To summarise my school years, I think my education, from start to finish, had been on a par with my spiritual instruction, received both in the Cottage and Village church: formal and rather indifferent. In spite of this, and as the hymn I chose to open this chapter with states, I *did* learn to become "steadfast" and "strong", although never really "wise"!

I was also to learn, on the many future occasions when I stood "all alone", that I was being shielded by a "mighty Hand". Valuable lessons!

CHAPTER SEVEN:
Troubled Teens

Dear Lord and Father of mankind,
Forgive our foolish ways.
...
Breathe through the heats of our desire
Thy coolness and Thy balm;
Let sense be dumb, let flesh retire;
Speak through the earthquake, wind and fire,
O still small voice of calm!
JOHN GREENLEAF WHITTIER (1807–92)

PART I: GROWING PAINS

My teenage years did not get off to a very favourable start. The fact that I had now 'become a woman' brought with it increasing self-consciousness and a sense of isolation.

I became, like most teenagers even under the best of circumstances, subject to what might nowadays be described as 'nervous tension'. Neither of the matrons tolerated these episodes of mine. The stock remark was almost always "When you get to *my* age, *then* you can admit to 'having nerves'!" At this time they would both have been about forty-plus, so it was a simple case of bottling up my feelings.

The result of this was that I do not think I ever really came to terms with the painful transition from child to stable adult.

I was not a particularly attractive young person, as increasing shortsightedness forced me to wear the detested spectacles constantly. My hair, which if left to its own curly devices could have been pretty, was routinely hacked at, once every six weeks or so, by a local hairdresser who charged about 2s. 6d. per visit. My long, athletically-shaped legs were my bane, as the reader already knows!

Although I was never troubled with that scourge of the teens – acne – I at least wanted to guard against it! Someone at school had seen an advertisement, possibly in a magazine such as *Valentine*, which was one of the new and exclusively teenage magazines that had just arrived on the scene. This advertisement was for Valderma soap, which was guaranteed to keep any incipient spots at bay. I think I shared my first tablet of this soap with another girl in the Village.

Something that will astound today's young people is that I was not permitted to use deodorants. I was an extremely active girl and very aware of the need to be clean and sweet-smelling at all times. However, the matrons told me that "if you wash yourself PROPERLY, you won't need such nonsense!"

'Washing properly' in those days generally meant using strong-smelling carbolic soap and having handfuls of soda thrown into the bath water.

Later on, though, my Christmas pillowcases would contain bath salts or bars of Knights Castile and Imperial Leather. What joy! Sometimes I was given soap and talcum powder for my birthday. I think these luxury items were sent by the aunty and uncle, who were young and consequently more 'with it' where teenage cosmetic needs were concerned.

Then there was the embarrassing matter of… body hair, and how to get rid of it. I can recall smuggling a half-used tube of Veet-O into the Cottage, although I can't remember who gave it to me – probably a school chum with an older sister. The cream was applied with a plastic spatula, but the smell of it was *so* ghastly and the results so patchy that I threw it into the dustbin.

Whilst I was on holiday with the aunty and uncle one summer,

I thought that perhaps uncle's razor might be able to deal with the problem of my faintly hispid limbs. I locked myself in the bathroom (forbidden, both in the Cottage *and* on holiday!) and scraped painfully away at my arms and legs. Then I dried them and applied talcum powder – lovely!

Unfortunately, whilst doing this, another part of my anatomy caught my eye, and I picked up uncle's razor again. So far, so good, though a great deal more tricky since my eyesight was poor and my glasses kept steaming up, so I had to remove them. When I had completed my task, I washed out the razor and returned it to the bathroom cupboard. "Now, I'm going to do what I've seen uncle do after *he* shaves!" I said to myself, and reached for his bottle of aftershave lotion... It was one of the few mistakes in my life that I did *not* make more than once!

It has already been seen that I did not have a great deal of self-confidence. I think this was because I had become a nonentity in the Cottage by now. I was not one of the little ones, to be petted and played with; neither was I what I *should* have been: the Oldest Girl, the one whom all the other children looked up to. The matrons' increasingly possessive attitude towards the sisters had taken care of that. I was 'in the way', and as such the almost daily butt of quite unnecessary put-downs.

When the matrons told me that I would "never amount to much" or "be any good to anyone", I suppose I could have retorted, "What can you expect from such a lost beginning?" However, although Charles Dickens was one of my favourite authors, I had not yet travelled as far as Mugby Junction!

When a young person grows up in an atmosphere of being constantly undervalued, he or she becomes scarred – for life. Take it from someone who, as we say in Greece, has a diploma in the subject!

In retrospect, I am certain that what enabled me to cope with those final, deeply unhappy years in the Cottage was my ability to lose myself in my hobbies of knitting and reading. It was ironic that both of these had been carefully fostered in me by the very women who now thought so little of me.

Over the years, I made several attempts at establishing some sort of rapport with Miss C, as she had always remained my favourite; but it was time wasted.

The two main problems I faced at all times were injustice and indifference. They were to rear their unlovely heads, many years later, in yet another ostensibly 'family-orientated, Christian environment'.

PART II: TEENAGE LIFE IN THE VILLAGE

Dr Barnardo's was not very well-equipped to cope with the emergence of that troublesome phenomenon, the teenager, but then, was *any*body at that time? Even today, I still hear older women, from both sides of the Atlantic, insisting that "of course, Elvis Presley started it all!" I cannot comment on this as when he first appeared on the scene I was too young and had neither heard nor seen him.

The trainee nursery nurses and assistant cottage matrons, however, would certainly have played his records. Even in America, Elvis or, 'Elvis the Pelvis' as he soon became known, was not considered 'respectable', for two reasons. His stage performance was disapproved of to such an extent that during the early years he was only ever filmed from the waist up! In addition to this, his singing style was too reminiscent of what was then called coloured people's music – so much so that many American radio stations refused to air his records!

If a 'normal' family outside the Village experienced problems dealing with one or two teenagers, just imagine how difficult it must have been for the rather staid Village adults to meet the needs of upwards of a hundred or so of us!

Let us take a peep into my diary for 1961, which was, as the reader knows, my final year in the Village: "Tuesday, 3rd of January – Went to a 'Social'. Won a comb. Danced with the Colonel – saw some good boys!"

These 'social' events were introduced especially for teenagers and were held in the large assembly hall at Mossford School. The boys would be clad in regulation-style grey suits, or blazers and long or knee-length trousers of grey or navy. Ties would have been obligatory, I am sure, and their hair was slicked back with Brylcreem. The rather 'common', but extremely fashionable 'DA' could only remain a dream as far as most of our Village boys were concerned, and I certainly do not remember seeing it at a Village social. My younger readers should approach their grandparents in order to find out what 'D.A.' meant. It was yet another item on the list of 'not-respectables'!

Mossford School, rear view

We girls wore pretty 'dirndl' skirts (I made mine during school needlework lessons) and pastel-coloured blouses, or prim frocks. Over these outfits would be worn cardigans, which were usually hand knitted. White ankle socks and black or tan 'casuals' completed this modest ensemble. Needless to say, we were all on our best behaviour!

The sort of music we danced to? Very formal. The Veleta, a Strauss waltz or two, maybe the Gay Gordons, but definitely *no* 'pop'! To be chosen to dance with the Colonel, as I had been on one heady occasion, was considered a very great honour indeed. A fortunate boy might be observed, shyly 'leading out' the Colonel's lady. You can be certain that his pals would *not* let him forget this 'honour' in a hurry!

There were party games, too, such as Pass the Parcel and Musical Chairs. I probably won my comb in this last, as I was a nippy runner and had sharp elbows! A wonderful time would have been had by all, but as I was rather diffident when grown-ups were around, I usually only got as far as smirking and fluttering my eyelashes at the 'good boys' referred to in my diary!

"MONDAY 10th and WEDNESDAY 12th APRIL: Cross-country heats and Final. Good fun in the Forest!"

The "Forest" mentioned in my diary was Hainault, and this was a most prestigious occasion.

Here again, the Colonel officiated, and I used to have a photograph of him standing at the finishing line, stopwatch in one hand, shooting stick in the other, as he timed the first lads past the post. He is immaculately dressed in an expensive light trench coat, 'country' cords, peaked cap and stout brogues. By his side is Susie, his pet bull terrier, of whom I was mortally afraid.

I had developed this photograph myself at the newly-introduced Camera Club. This was also held at Mossford School. I can still recall the dizzy sense of achievement that I felt at being instructed into the mysteries of photography and actually handling the end results! All us youngsters who attended these classes were presented with a brand new Kodak 'Reflex' camera. It was my first valuable possession, and I was to use it for several years, until I left it on a beach somewhere in the West Country!

But to return to Hainault Forest and the cross-country event. The "fun in the Forest" referred to was a very innocent affair, and only consisted of shouting at our favourite boys as they flew past us girls, and, as far as I was concerned, seeing how many trees I could climb.

"MONDAY 24th APRIL:
Went to oculists to be fitted up for (I hope!) fancy specs."

The oculist was Odell's in Barkingside High Street. The fancy specs were ordered by Head Office as I was due to go out into the world in July. They were a rather gruesome 'butterfly' style, which was the mode for all females at that time. The colour was dark red. I thought I looked the 'bee's knees' in them, but the matrons prudently put them away "for safety"!

Because of my acute self-consciousness, I did not take a great deal of interest in prevailing teenage fashions. The only item of 'girlie' clothing I can recall ever *really* wanting was a 'Poodle' skirt. Over and over, I used to say to myself, "Oh, I *wish* I had the legs to wear one of those!" These skirts were brightly coloured and made from a rather heavy material (was it felt?) which stood out all round the wearer. At least two starched white 'paper-nylon' half-slips contributed to its 'lampshade' effect. A large fluffy 'poodle' was appliquéd onto this skirt, and it wore a glittery collar. Attached to this collar was a real chain dog's lead, which was fastened close to the waist with some sort of clasp. This skirt was so startlingly modish that I don't think any of our Village girls ever wore one, at least not in the Village!

My one attempt at being fashionable began and ended in a day. For my sixteenth birthday, the aunty sent me a pair of extremely dashing blue-and-white striped 'pedal-pushers' – a *real* teenage 'must have' of the day. I was enraptured and vividly recall my joy as I put them on. White ankle socks, buckled casual shoes, beautifully hand-knitted 'cardie' and a blouse comprised the remainder of this outfit. I cannot remember that the matrons made any comment at the time; they probably knew full well that, since our cottage was next door to Cairns

House and the redoubtable Miss G, I would meet her sooner or later. She would be more than able to deal with the situation!

I walked proudly out of the cottage gate and made my way to the Big Green, to strut my stuff (I am using an up-to-date teenage expression, for a change!) in front of any boys who might be in the vicinity.

Alas, I bumped straight into Miss G! She was *furious* and ordered me to "return to your cottage *immediately* and take off those *disgusting* trousers!"

Tearfully, I obeyed, and the pedal-pushers were laid aside for when I left the Village. There was no comment from the matrons!

There used to be a magazine called *Tit-Bits* in those days and on the front there would be photographs of young girls wearing swimsuits. I cannot say that I took much notice of their faces, or their bodies for that matter. However, I *was* intrigued when some of them were depicted wearing bikinis.

By today's regrettably 'anything goes' standards, this type of swimwear was exceedingly modest and the belly button was often discreetly covered. When the aunty bought me a pretty flowered and frilled bikini, I was horrified! I flatly refused to display so much of my body, although I definitely had the figure for it in those days! It was only when I went to live and work in Greece that I became confident enough to spend summer weekends wearing next to nothing on the beach.

The popular jeans and checked shirt were not often worn by Village teenagers. I suppose they were, like Elvis Presley, considered a rather vulgar American 'import', even though they were attractive and very practical. Our teenage boys wore either baggy khaki shorts and sandals during the summer (grey flannel trousers and ordinary lace-up shoes in the winter) unless they played in cricket matches, when the regulation 'ducks' were worn. On looking back over the years, I think our boys had the worst of it fashion-wise, and I can well remember the sensation caused when, as I wrote in my diary, "S wore a *new* jumper" to the Club! It was banded with brightly patterned stripes, and he became the centre of attraction. There just seemed to be no acceptable 'middle course' for boys. Conscription was ending and 'Teddy boy' suits were all the rage, at least in the East End of London. Under no circumstances, however, was such attire permitted to be worn by our lads. The only other mode at that period was the smart-casual style of sports shirt and tie, worn with beautifully pressed cotton drill trousers and maybe a pair of the 'new' moccasin shoes. This vogue would, I think, have been condemned as being "too sissy" by most of our red-blooded Village boys!

My matrons repeatedly told me that "when you start earning your *own* money, you will have the right to choose what you wear!" and, of course, they were perfectly right. But I do not remember ever thanking them for these constant reminders!

As a final 'fashion note', I want to mention something rather curious. I was almost always dressed in blue, in all its various shades apart from bright turquoise. I did not like this colour and have no idea, to this day, who first thought up the notion. Maybe the aunty? Most of my knitted cardigans and jumpers; the 'knife' or 'box' pleated skirts; shorts; frocks; and even swimsuits were, save for one or two exceptions, all blue.

It was only when I was permitted to choose the material for my 'leaving-the-Village' frock that I felt courageous enough to select the colour I *really* liked: a bright peony-red floral mix. I selected this from an array of materials on offer at the school needlework class, and it was looked upon as being a rather bold choice. I received quite a few uncomplimentary comments at the time I made this choice, especially from the matrons. "Well! What can you *expect* from Susan Plumb? She had always been a 'Notice Me!'" was one of the less hurtful ones.

Music especially geared for teenagers took some time to infiltrate into Village life. Whenever I got the chance, I would tune in to the pleasantly nasal-sounding voice of Brian Matthew as he introduced "Easy Beat, your Sunday Best!" This, however, would be guiltily switched off if one of the matrons (or a known tell-tale) approached. As with all other forms of entertainment, pop programmes were forbidden on the Day of Rest, although the matrons relented later on when they bought a television. Suddenly, it was "all right" to watch *Sunday Night at the London Palladium*. Nothing sways us so much as self-interest!

The Head Office gradually relaxed its rules about us teenagers having fun, when they let us have our own Club (hermetically closed on Sundays, of course).

It was held on the top floor of our big clothing store, which is now called Linney House. We were allotted a small 'dance room' furnished with a few chairs. It contained the necessary record player which, again, would almost certainly have been the popular Dansette. We were also given (or indeed, might have been allowed to choose for ourselves, but my memory fails me here) a selection a 45-rpm records which were in the current 'Hit Parade'. One of the most popular singers was Cliff Richard. He was never an idol of mine, but his diction was usually so clear that I was able to take down nearly all his songs in shorthand.

My 'dreamboats' were, not surprisingly, both blond. John Leyton, with his brilliant blue eyes and throaty rendering of 'Johnny, Remember Me' used to find me starry eyed and draped over the record player, oblivious to everyone. The heart-stopping, sulky good looks of Adam Faith as he sang 'What D'ya Want?' or 'Poor Me' really 'sent' me. That fascinating 'hiccup' in his voice also caused me to miss many a shot in the table tennis room close by!

Neil Sedaka and The Everly Brothers were prime favourites as they were fun to sing along with. Girls who could jive would whirl around the floor, either with a boy (lucky lasses!) or a girlfriend, to Bill Haley and the Comets' 'Rock Around the Clock', the strident tones of Gene Vincent's 'Be-Bop-A-Lula!' or Buddy Holly's 'Peggy-Sue'.

I think Emil Ford was the only coloured British singer at that time, apart from the extremely handsome Cy Grant (who did not sing regular pop and had his own television programme, if my memory serves me correctly). Emil Ford and the Checkmates had an instant hit with 'What Do You Want to Make Those Eyes at Me For?' Someone later told me that he played at the Ilford Palais too, but I don't think Barnardo children were allowed to go *there*.

After I had left the Village, Danny William's beautiful rendering of 'Moon River' entered the Hit Parade and remained there for some weeks. The Village boys seemed to prefer gutsy records, such as Duane Eddy's 'Forty Miles of Bad Road' or Sandy Nelson's tediously repetitive 'Drums Are my Beat'. Connie Francis was one of the best-loved American girl singers, but *my* eyes used to light up when the diminutive 'Little Miss Dynamite' (Brenda Lee) belted out 'Speak to Me, Pretty!' I could not understand how someone so small could have such a powerful voice.

I think it was at the Club that most of us girls learnt how to do the tricky 'hand jive'. I never became an adept exponent of this art, as I always wanted to introduce alternative gestures, but I enjoyed watching the experts. The lights in the dance room were kept full on at all times, as I recall, no doubt to discourage 'smooching'; not even to such romantic numbers as Pat Boone's 'April Love' or Cliff's 'Travellin' Light'. An assistant master or the curate was ever-present, to see that we toed the boring line of propriety!

I can also remember sitting on the chilly iron steps of the fire escape, taking a hesitant puff at my first cigarette – a Wills Woodbine, I think. Fortunately, I did not enjoy it enough to make it a habit, although I know that several of the boys had been smoking from about the age of fourteen.

The games of billiards and snooker were also played at our Club, and were extremely popular with both boys and girls. I became quite a skilful player at both these games, and had been taught by David, a boy in the cottage next to mine. In my first 'real' snooker game, I beat him into a cocked hat, and I don't think it was just beginner's luck either, although he insisted that it was!

Whenever we youngsters got the chance, we would make for the 'Rec', which was how most people described the recreation ground in Cranbrook Road. We did not do much there, as I recall. The boys would either wander round 'playing big' with their fags, or kick footballs about on the pitch. We girls would sit on the swings and discuss which boys we liked the look of. There would have been very little 'dirty talk' in those days, and of course no alcoholic drinks! A large bottle of Tizer or ginger beer might occasionally be shared between us, though.

Coffee bars had not yet arrived on the scene in Barkingside at that time. If they had, no Barnardo youngster would have been allowed to enter one anyway. The place *I* would like to have spent time (and pocket money!) in was Rossi's ice cream parlour, which I have already referred to.

Going to the 'flicks' at night unaccompanied by an adult, was forbidden, although Saturday matinees were much enjoyed. If I was good, or to use yet another of the matrons' stock phrases, "less objectionable than usual", I was permitted to join the eager crowd. My brightest memories are of watching Tommy Steele in *The Duke Wore Jeans* (in which I think he sang the song 'Photograph my Baby') and *The Tommy Steele Story*, which told of his meteoric rise to fame. Heady stuff in those days!

My first brush with boy-girl relationships came when I heard one of the girls in the Cottage talking about how far she let a boy 'go' with her. I can remember feeling shocked and slightly unclean. The reason for this was that earlier experiences had made me feel that talking about the body and its functions, especially my *own* body, was 'dirty'.

I recall telling Matron C, in a suitably hushed voice, that I had overheard one of the girls talking about "being dirty with boys"! (Matron was ironing at the time; I can see her now, with her iron poised over the board. She is looking hard at me as I stumble out the words.) She asked me to "explain *exactly* what you mean", but I was unable to do so as I had not seen anything. I have no idea of what she made of all this, but the subject was not referred to again, at least not in *my* presence. I only ever had one genuine boyfriend whilst I was in the Village. He met me at an Inter-homes sports day, when the boys from Goldings descended upon the Village.

Goldings Technical School was in Hertfordshire, and boys went there to learn various trades such as printing and carpentry. There was also a flourishing and well-trained Brass band. The boys would 'open' Village summer events by parading round the Big Green in their smart uniforms, but I can't remember any of the tunes they played. I am certain, however, that John Philip Sousa's rousing marches must have appeared on the programme.

One of the lads had taken a shine to me. He asked his mate, a friend of mine who had lived in the cottage opposite Clement, for my name, and I was thrilled to receive my first love letter in due course. It was at this time that I began to get *really* angry at having my letters opened and read by the matrons.

In those fairly innocent days, smitten boys and girls would write coded messages on the backs of their envelopes. SWALK (sealed with a loving kiss) and BOLTOP (better on lips than on paper) were two that *my* boyfriend used. I think I can remember putting 1.4.3. (I.love.you) on one or two of mine.

Very passionate young swains, however, with rather more than just kisses on their minds, might send their girls the saucily-acronymic demand to 'BURMA'! I wonder how many of my more mature readers will remember *this* one. My pen pal and I only met on a couple of occasions, before I left the Village and he moved on from Goldings.

I had been a tomboy for so many years that boys never really posed a threat to me, and apart from two other notable occasions, I treated them as chums. The first of these notable occasions was when I developed a passion for the son of a couple who had recently taken over one of the double cottages on the Reception Green. Clive was very attractive, and the Village girls almost came to blows over who would appropriate him. However, he took no interest in poor, frumpy me at all, and any dreams I might have had of us exchanging kisses soon faded into unhappy oblivion!

The other boy, Ted, was a *real* tearaway – the despair of even the strictest of the Village masters. I fell head over heels in love with him, and was always being teased by the girls. Here again, though, I was to fail miserably for, apart from the odd wink at me, I was passed over for the more attractive girls, and I never became one of his 'conquests'!

I experienced my first 'taste of the fruit' when I was sixteen. Here is my diary note:

SATURDAY THE 15TH OF JULY 1961 – ST SWITHINS DAY:
Inter-homes sports. Went with a super boy called Frank. He was *very intimate* with me!

Hold on, reader! Do not be alarmed. Let me explain exactly what occurred.

The sports had ended, and Frank and I wandered down the leafy lane that lead to Barkingside Station, from where he would commence his return journey to Goldings. Once inside the station, Frank steered me solicitously to the extreme end of the platform, away from any prying eyes, and started to kiss me. I was not particularly responsive as I had never engaged in this sort of thing before.

All of a sudden, his hand crept up the back of my white piqué blouse, which was worn 'box' fashion outside my dirndl skirt. Perspiring heavily and breathing in short, sharp bursts, Frank then tried to undo my brassiere. As my back was by now firmly positioned against the station fence, I was unable to escape. However, he was not very successful. At this highly-charged moment, the train came along... and whisked him away! I drifted out of the station and made my way back to the Village. I was on cloud nine. At last I could hold my head high amongst the other girls! A GOLDINGS BOY, one of those Lords of Creation, had found me attractive enough to be 'intimate' with me! I lived off that dream for days; although in retrospect, I wouldn't mind betting that he had only done it for a 'dare'. I wasn't much of a catch!

Being a teenager in those days was very difficult, and not just for me. The reader is already aware that human biology was not taught in my school; few of us were taught anything about what to expect as our bodies changed, and 'hormones' were quite unknown to us! Girls were merely exhorted to be "extra-clean during your time of the month". In some cottages, this included a ban on washing the hair, which I am sure will raise a few eyebrows amongst my young lady readers! And, of course, there was "no going near the boys"!

The only naked males I ever remember seeing during my early teens were in the lurid photographs contained in such books as Lord Russell's *The Scourge of the Swastika*, and the equally alarming *Camp on Blood Island* – an illustrated exposé of Japanese war crimes. In those comparatively early post-war days, bookshops and newsagents held a seemingly inexhaustible supply of books which gave unexpurgated details of torture camps in Germany. There were also the deeply disturbing diaries, written by our poor British men who were forced to work on the notorious Burma–Siam Railway. The name 'Changhi' can still no doubt evoke powerful and frightening memories for many of today's ex-POW men.

I was particularly drawn to the sketches of different methods of torture. Even today, I can feel the tears pricking my eyelids as I think of how I used to pore over those dreadful pictures. Why *was* I so unable to resist their gloomy attraction? Were there any parallels to be drawn between the illustrated suffering and my own increasing unhappiness? Did I feel soothed in any way, by the fact that what I was looking at, what the poor people were suffering, was indeed worse than anything *I* had ever experienced? I am not sure that I want any answers to these questions, thank you all the same!

My teenage reading reached its cheerless peak when I became possessed of two books which might, even today, be considered "not very suitable for young people". The first was *Mein Kampf* by Adolf Hitler. I found this autobiography totally absorbing, although I was really too young to take it all in. It was stolen from me, under very distressing circumstances, two years after I left the Village.

The second book was to prove the most terrifying story I have *ever* read. *Burn, Witch, Burn* was written by an American, Abe Merritt. It was acknowledged as being "one of the greatest tales of horror and fantasy fiction ever written". Merritt was ranked with Edgar Allan Poe and Algernon Blackwood as "one of the great masters of the supernatural".

It is, I am sure, unnecessary to mention that I kept *this* book well hidden from the matrons! However, the lurid war crime stories were read quite openly by many of us teenagers, and were avidly swapped between us, both in the Village and at school.

I have recently been fortunate enough to get hold of a much-battered copy of Pedigree Books' version of *Burn, Witch, Burn*, which was originally priced at 2s. 6d. This was two years ago, and I am *still* trying to pluck up the courage to read it again. Madam Mandilip is, for certain, going to be capable of chilling my blood all over again!

PART III: LOSING FRIENDS

For many years, Dr Barnardo's sent children out to Canada and Australia to "make a new start in life". In theory, this was a splendid idea. In practice, however, many of these children's lives were to be blighted because their new foster parents had not been well chosen.

I am not in a position to comment at length on the rights and wrongs of their system. Suffice to say that I *do* know that it was sometimes considered 'expedient' to separate brothers and sisters, and even twins. In many cases, these children would not see each other again. It is a highly-emotive subject altogether, and, in my opinion, will unfortunately remain a 'black mark' against Barnardo's old system of 'selection'.

Thank goodness those bad old days have been left far behind! Nowadays, everything possible is done to make sure that families are not separated unless it is absolutely necessary, when 'access' cases are dealt with very sensitively.

Because no real mum or dad ever visited me, I used to get very excited when I heard that children were being "picked to go to Australia". I had dreams about how much happier my life would be once I got away from my hated cottage, to a land of sunshine and opportunities.

Then came the year when one of my very best Village chums informed me that *she* had been chosen to join the Australia contingent, and would be leaving within a week or two. I was DEVASTATED. We had grown up together, we had shared the same passion for field sports and swimming, and were the same age. We really *were* like sisters. *Why* couldn't I go out with her?

This is the most painful part of my story, the most long-lasting and bitter of *all* my memories. It was only when I was living in Greece that I was able to put into words exactly how I felt at this time:

THE PROMISED LAND
"Goodbye!　　　　Goodbye!
We're sailing today
To a new life – on a big boat!"
I watched them go, then turned away;
Tears fell on my navy-blue coat.

"Goodbye!　　　　Goodbye!
We're flying away
To Australia – on a big plane!"
I didn't reply; I had nothing to say,
Though I knew I'd not see them again.

"Hello!　　　　Hello!
What's this? Why, tears!
Don't be jealous; they're orphans, you know.
Each year we select and send off the best;
You're too naughty, that's why *you* can't go!"

"Don't lie!   Don't lie!"
I frowned and I sulked.
(I couldn't tell why, but I *knew*...
That wasn't the reason I never became
One of the fortunate few).

"Aha!   Aha!"
What's this? An album;
Photographs taken in faraway places.
I look at my chums (and those I don't know);
They have one thing in common: white faces!

"Oh no!   Oh no!
It *can't* be true!"
(I was young, and did not understand
That it was not my behaviour, but colour
Which barred *me* from the Promised Land!)

Two-faced!   Two-faced!
The society that condemns
Say, Hitler, and his 'Perfect Breed',
Then by colour, race or health determines
The fate of us children in need!

As I mentioned, in Chapter Two, some mothers would come to the Village on Saturdays and take their children out for the day. I still have painful memories of how *I* felt as I gazed longingly out of the playroom window on these visiting days. The lucky little girls would be *so* excited when mummy rang the doorbell. They would rap on the window and then run to the front door whilst struggling into their coats and chattering happily. This feeling of missing out stayed with me until I left the Village.

Sometimes parents, most particularly mothers who had either married or remarried, would approach Dr Barnardo's and request to be put in touch with their children again, after years of not being in contact with them at all.

I lost another friend of mine in this manner. She simply disappeared one day, and I did not see her again until forty years later. The story she told me, of how her mother had reclaimed her, was a horrifying tale of callous indifference, exploitation and abuse. That she survived her terrible ordeal and is able to give her children and grandchildren the love which she was never shown by her own mother, I consider to be little short of a miracle.

These errant 'mothers' were unconcerned about their offspring whilst they were growing up in the Village. However, as soon as the child became of an age to go out to work, the woman would suddenly display an interest in its welfare. An interview would be arranged to meet the youngster, and then the mother would probably spin a hard-luck story of how difficult it had been for her to keep and care for her child, how much she still loved it, and now wanted to "make up for the lost years".

The reason for this sudden interest in their children, whom they had ignored for so many years, was quite obvious in many cases: the mother wanted an extra wage-earner in the family. Another wage packet, no matter how small, would have been an extremely useful addition to most working-class families at that time. In my opinion, this is a despicable form of emotional blackmail, because many of us children in Barnardo's were desperate to know who our real parents were, and why we never saw them.

Several years after I left the Village, the woman who had given birth to me contacted Dr Barnardo's, who then got in touch with me. Apparently, Mrs P was most anxious for us to meet, and I was asked if I would like Head Office to arrange a meeting.

I cannot remember what my exact reply to this offer was, but I *do* know that I had no inclination at all to being put in touch with her.

For my entire childhood Mrs P had remained stonily indifferent to my welfare, until I became of an age to, presumably, be of use to her. I have no regrets about the decision I made at the time. All my sympathies are reserved for those youngsters who were reclaimed and whose lives were to be subsequently damaged by the experience.

I have mentioned before, and think that it bears repeating, that many of the children in the Village *were* 'lucky'. They were brought up in an atmosphere of compassionate solicitude for their welfare, which enabled them to develop as normal, well-adjusted young people, fully able to take their place in the challenging world outside the Village.

CHAPTER EIGHT:
Being 'Moved On'

Be Thou my vision, O Lord of my heart.

.....

Be Thou my great Father, and I Thy true son;
Be Thou in me dwelling, and I with Thee one.

IRISH c. 8th century
Trans. MARY BURNE (1880–1931)
Versified by ELEANOR HULL (1860–1935)

This was one my favourite 'boys' hymns', and I used to start singing it with great gusto.

When we reached verse two, though, my voice would falter at the last two lines. I am sure that it was because I felt, instinctively, my vulnerability as a girl. Oh, why *couldn't* I have been born a BOY, and become a *real* son to a *real* father?!

Fate had decided otherwise, however. I was just a rather plain lass of sixteen. No last-minute miracle had occurred; no long-lost father had arrived at the Cottage to claim me. Neither had my brothers, Carl and Tony, put in an appearance yet.

I felt abandoned... and extremely frightened.

PART I: 'FAREWELLING'

Before teenagers left the Village to go out into the world, they went through a process called 'farewelling'.

In my day, this took place in the Headquarters at Stepney Causeway. My memories of what precisely took place have proved so vague that I have been compelled to enlist the help of a member of the (now called) Making Connections Department!

The routine was that, together with a group of other youngsters from the Village, and dressed in my very best, I attended this auspicious ceremony. We were each presented with a brand new Bible, a suitcase, a copy of *The Guild Messenger* and (I am certain of *this!*) a Book token. *The Guild Messenger* was what nowadays would probably be called an 'in-house magazine'. It gave up-to-date news about what was going on in the Barnardo world, not only in the United Kingdom, but also Canada and Australia where, as I have already mentioned, many children had settled. It still flourishes today. The dates and venues of any forthcoming reunions are also given.

REUNIONS
The sounds of welcome; conversation,
Recalling far-off years.
Fellowship and celebration;
The laughter… and the tears!

We talk so much, we all have tales
To tell of long ago;
"Remember this?" "Remember that?"
A glance; a smile; "Hello!"

Old photographs show many faces,
Some with us, some now absent.
We point out once-familiar places
And wonder where the time went!

Strolling through the grounds at noon
In friendly groups, and taking
Photographs of Church and pals;
New memories in the making.

But, pause a while, and bring to mind
Those who have passed away.
Their youthful faces, fresh, unlined
Are with us still today.

Turn the lights out! Say "Goodbye!"
Another year has gone.
But, shaking hands, our hopes are high
For the *next* Reunion!

After the presentation ceremony a speech was given by, I think, General Sir Arthur Smith. He was a very great personage in Dr Barnardo's. He was also an extremely unassuming and gentle person, as truly 'great' people very often are.

There was a celebratory tea, but here again my memory does not extend to describing the menu. Nor do I remember having my photograph taken, but here it is...

I am wearing the dress I mentioned in the previous chapter. The collar took *ages* to get right during needlework class at school as it was a 'double' one. By the time I had finished it, the needlework teacher had to have it laundered before it could be sewn onto the frock!

My haircut is dire, and my expression, in spite of the lopsided grin, is rather apprehensive. I *can* remember that I flatly refused to be photographed wearing my new butterfly spectacles; they were probably being held carefully in my lap.

In addition to the Bible, suitcase and book token, I was also kitted out with new clothes. The most expensive item was "1 Raincoat: £4. 7s. 6d." A good pair of 'sensible' shoes i.e. low-heeled, black courts cost £3. 3s. 11d. Two day frocks were priced at £1. 14s. 6d. A "suspender belt and one pair of stockings" set Barnardo's back 5s. 10d. and 4s. 11d. respectively. The entire leaving outfit cost the immense sum of £15.

14s. 6d. (£15.52) and included a toilet bag with contents. In retrospect, I am positive that the matrons would have thought, and might indeed have said, for all I know, that I was not worth this large amount being spent on me.

I have a record of all my wordly wealth here,too. Would you like to see it?

- Post Office savings (This was the reward-for-honesty money referred to in Part I of Chapter Five.) . . . . 5s. 0d (25p).

- Savings Stamps . . . . 11s. 6d (61p).

- Pocket money . . . . 10s. 0d (50p).

This princely sum was to be carefully husbanded until such time as I received my first grown-up wage packet.

The next important event during my final days at the Village, was the 'Leaving interview'. This was held in the large study at Cairns House and was conducted by Miss G, to whom the reader has already been introduced. I think the general idea of this 'pep talk' was to prepare me for entry into society by giving me a few pointers as to *who* I was and how I was to behave. Miss G's manner was uncompromising from the outset, and as I knew she had never liked me, I was immediately on the defensive.

She commenced the talk by giving me a few exceedingly guarded details about my parentage. My 'father' had been "a coloured American" and was "not interested" in me. I would not be having any contact with the 'mother' (much I cared for *that*!). Apparently, she was "not interested" either.

I would be 'boarded out' with the aunt and uncle I had been spending my school holidays with. At no time were questions such as "What would you *really* like to do, Susan?" or "Are you happy with our decision?" asked. So much for my dream of staying in London and studying to become a journalist!

I gave a sigh, shifted from one foot to the other and then, taking a deep breath, blurted out (and I can remember *this* part vividly) "But, what about my *brothers*? When am I going to meet *them*?"

There was a cold, strained silence; then Miss G dropped her bombsheath. She told me that I had no brothers, no relatives at all – at least none who were prepared to acknowledge me. However, I stood my ground and insisted that I had been told, over and over again, that I had two brothers; their names were Carl and Tony. When I was older, I would meet them. They were white and were living with our 'mother'.

In no uncertain terms, Miss G made it quite clear that these brothers had never existed and, as I had no family, it was entirely up to me to "make something" of myself.

The effect this long-standing and gratuitous lie had on my feelings of happy expectation and confidence was catastrophic. I was leaving the only home I had ever known, to go out into a world for which I had not been prepared, either spiritually or emotionally. In addition to this, I had now been informed that there would be no joyous meeting with the brothers I had dreamed of for so many years.

It was a loss from which I have never truly recovered. It was like a death had taken place behind my back.

Thus ended my 'farewelling' from Dr Barnardo's Village Home at Barkingside.

PART II: LEAVING THE COTTAGE

I think the loss I suffered when I was told I had no brothers must also have permanently affected my ability to remember exactly what occurred on the day I left Clement Cottage.

As I write, one picture alone persists in drifting across my mind's eye. It is that of poor Jo, the crossing sweeper in Charles Dickens' *Bleak House*. Jo had the potential to be a good little boy if only someone had reached out and told him he was valuable. Instead of this, he was forever being ignored, hassled, or roughly told to "move on!"

Although I was fairly pleased about going to live with the aunty and uncle mentioned in previous chapters, I dreaded the prospect of actually leaving the Village. Not the Cottage; I wanted to get right away from *there*. I had been unhappy in it for years.

However, the decision *had* been made; my farewelling *had* taken place, and I was indeed about to be 'moved on'.

In Part I of Chapter Two, I stated in the footnote that I had recently come into possession of several additional papers.

The letter that caused me considerable distress was contained in a Barnardo report on a school leavers' discussion which took place on the 3rd of July 1961, which was two weeks before I was due to leave Fairlop. I was not invited to attend this meeting.

The part that upset me was a remark made by the Welfare Officer, Miss 'Q', who was to 'guide' my future career. She wrote:

> "I am doubtful if Mrs 'M' (the aunt) and Susan will agree and settle down for long."

In another letter Miss Q made it abundantly clear that she did:

> "…not want Susan working in Mrs M's office (nor does her husband); we know it would not answer."

Neither, apparently, did Mrs M want me working in the same place as her husband, although I would have been in the typing pool and he on the factory floor!

Is it any wonder, then, that I was upset when I read the above? It was patently obvious, almost fifty years too late, that I should never have been boarded out with this couple. For younger readers, I should perhaps have explained that boarding out simply meant that one lived with a couple, as part of the family. A portion of any wages were retained by the couple to cover board and lodging expenses, which of course included meals.

My leaving the Cottage could certainly have been described as the non-event of 1961! I do not remember any 'celebration tea' such as those which took place in other cottages. Indeed, I am sure none took place. I should imagine that the only feeling, certainly where the matrons and sisters were concerned, was one of immense relief. They were at last getting rid of a girl who had been a thorn in their flesh for years.

I am sure that my situation could have been ameliorated if the Welfare Officer's misgivings had been investigated, or I could at least have achieved a friendly rapport with her. Unfortunately, although very kind, she was not a well-chosen guide for a troubled youngster like me. She was old (all of 45-ish!), besides being much-wrinkled and very plain. She wore sensible brogues and fussy felt hats. I felt all the teenager's painful embarrassment at being seen with such a frump. To cap it all, I had to deal with my problem of feeling uncomfortable with an older woman.

Nowadays, youngsters are much more fortunate. They get allotted buzzy young people to help pilot them through life's stormy seas. These people are given titles such as Buddy or Mate, and are usually dressed in jeans and trainers. They seem to have an inexhaustible energy for long walks and various sports. What is most important of all, they are trained to LISTEN; to deal with such diverse problems as adolescent insecurity, stress, low self-esteem and... what to wear to a rave! I admire them, and think they do a wonderful and valuable job.

The fact was, I resented my Welfare Officer's 'interference' in my life, and was unable to make a confidante of her. We were both caught up at the crossroads of change, and neither of us were prepared for the immense revolution that was beginning to take place in the minefield of Social Welfare.

For the very first time, young people were to be given a voice in how they felt they should be treated. Their opinions were being sought, listened to and acted upon, for their *own* benefit.

The ideal Welfare Officer for me, upon leaving the Village, would have been a middle-aged married man with a growing family. He would have been what is now called an excellent role model and the vital father figure I was so obviously in need of. However, it was not to be.

Somehow, I arrived at Paddington Station on the 11th of August 1961. My case had been sent on ahead, to "save her carrying it". I wore a bright, cap-sleeved summer frock, and as I settled myself into the second-class No Smoking carriage, I looked about me excitedly.

I had left the Village and the hated Cottage. At last! I was actually On my Way... to all sorts of adventures and, maybe, successes! Smashing!

I had no idea whatsoever that I was in fact about to enter a veritable 'war zone', for which I had not been prepared. With no emotional armour and no spiritual weapons, I would come face to face with a formidable foe. From now on, it was going to be the Great World against Susan Jane Plumb – that rather scatterbrained, well-meaning, but perilously vulnerable Barnardo kid.

The train pulled out of Paddington Station and I gave a little bounce of excitement as the offices and houses began to move rapidly past the window.

As we gathered speed, I was precipitated forward... to meet the inevitable, and inexorable, fate which awaited me.

CHAPTER NINE:
Of Things Spiritual

I think, when I read that sweet story of old,
When Jesus was here among men,
How He called little children as lambs to His fold,
I should like to have been with them then.
I wish that His hand had been placed on my head,
That His arm had been thrown around me;
And that I might have seen His kind look when He said:
Let the little ones come unto Me!
JEMIMA LUKE (1813–1906)

In parenthesis, I appreciate that non-Christians or, indeed, non-believers, might be inclined to skip this chapter. They may find its title off-putting. However, I beg them to reconsider and read on. The chapter is pivotal to the story of my early life, and its conclusion will, I hope, put everything into perspective. There! I *knew* you would accede to my request... Thank you!

I am going to commence with a brief glance through my school reports regarding the class subject entitled Religious Instruction. 'RI', as it has always been abbreviated by schoolchildren, was one of my three favourite lessons, the other two being English Language and English Literature. All my reports on the subject of RI are excellent, except for the one at term ending 1960. Here the teacher, who was also our form mistress, gave me a C-plus and wrote: "Must work hard if she is to reach the high level attainable by a girl of her intelligence". Not too bad, is it? Other teachers reported, "Very good. Has done a splendid year's work" (20th of July 1960); "Susan is quick and intelligent. She has done good, sound work all the term" (17th of December 1959); and "An intelligent girl; works quickly and well" (December 1958). The final report for summer 1961 reads "Has done a good year's work".

So the facts are indisputable. I *was* able to achieve at school, in spite of being unhappy at 'home'... *if* I put my mind to it!

Upon looking back, I believe that my enjoyment of Religious Instruction formed the solid rock on which my faith was built, although I was to endure many setbacks before I became absolutely certain of this fact.

PART I: THE VILLAGE CHURCH

The Church's one Foundation
Is Jesus Christ, her Lord.
SAMUEL JOHN STONE (1839–1900)

Dr Barnardo had the Village church built especially for children – '*his*' children. Without becoming too technical, I should like to mention a few interesting facts about it.

WANTED – A CHILDREN' S CHURCH

This was the wording of an appeal that Thomas John Barnardo made in January 1891.

There were at that time about one thousand girls in the Village, and none of the local churches were big enough to accommodate them all.

The original cost estimate for a church was £3,000, which Barnardo equated to forty shillings per sitting. A lady donor offered the amount required, but when actual bids were tendered, the lowest estimate was found to be almost £2,800 more. Dr Barnardo returned, cap in hand, to the benefactress and, after a nervous wait, she agreed to fund the full amount required.

The architect chosen for this job was a well-known London architect, Ebenezer Gregg. On Saturday the 25th of June 1892, a group of dignitaries and supporters gathered to watch a memorial stone being put in place by the generous donor. The lady requested that she remain anonymous. This stone, which can be seen in the entrance porch, reads: "This Church is dedicated to the Glory of God. In loving memory of her father and mother by their daughter."

Village Church

Dr Barnardo himself often spoke in the church. For his first sermon, given at the evening service on the 20th of August 1893, he took as his text Hebrews Chapter 12 verse 24: "And to Jesus the mediator of the new covenant, and to the blood of sprinkling, that speaketh better things than that of Abel."

The completed children's church was dedicated for worship in April 1894 by the Bishop of Colchester.

Dr Barnardo boasted, "Our children's worship is full of singing." And in the days of the Girls' Village the church had a choir of over three hundred girls who practised regularly. They also sang at the annual general meeting, which was held at the Royal Albert Hall.

Dr Barnardo was "willing to hear the cry of distress from whomsoever it may come", and so children were admitted from any religious background, or indeed none; though once admitted they were brought up in the Christian faith.

When the church was built, a space was left for an organ to be added, but it was not until 1935 that the present electric organ was made, by a company in Leyton called Spurden Rutt, and put into place.

The stained-glass windows in the 'east end' (though sharp-eyed visitors will notice that it is not actually pointing east!) were installed in 1936, after money was donated by members of Barnardo's council, Village staff, and as a memorial to an ex-member of staff.

Six hemispherical, chiming bells were hung in the tower when the church was first built. In 1926, two more bells were cast by the famous Whitechapel Foundry, which also tuned the other six. The bells received an overhaul in 2005, in time for the centenary service.

Banners in the church were made by The Young Helpers' League. These were children from more fortunate backgrounds all over the United Kingdom, who supported Dr Barnardo's Homes by collecting money. One of the cottages was called 'YHL' as a thank you to them.

Everything in the church is tailor-made to suit children. The pews are lower than normal, as are the stained-glass windows. Originally, the pews went right to the back of the church, where there was also a baptismal font. However, in 1968 these were removed and the area was refurbished.

PART II: DEATH OF DR BARNARDO

The day Thou gavest, Lord, is ended.

.....

Thy praise shall sanctify our rest...
JOHN ELLERTON (1826–93)

On the evening of the 19th of September 1905, at his home in Surbiton, Surrey, Dr Thomas John Barnardo leaned back in his chair and passed away. It had been his oft-repeated wish to "go off like a shot" and the Lord mercifully granted his desire.

When news of his death became public, there was a general outpouring of grief. Street boys waiting for the delivery of the evening paper were shocked into silence when they saw the single announcement: "Death of Dr Barnardo" in large, black letters.

From Dr Barnardo's lying-in at the Village church, to the subsequent funeral, the number of mourners attracted for a 'commoner' was not witnessed again until the burial of Sir Winston Churchill in 1965.

In the grounds of the Village, there is an eighteen-foot high memorial to Dr Barnardo. It was sculpted by Sir George Frampton R.A., who will be well known to the public as the creator of the 1912 statue of Peter Pan in Kensington Gardens. It is worth noting that Sir George gave his services "Without fee or reward".

(Author's note: I am indebted to Mrs Hilary Reeve, retired secretary of Barnardo's Prayer and Devotional Committee, for the above description of our church and the death of Dr Barnardo.)

I should like to conclude this section by quoting from *1000 Tales Worth Telling*, collected by Hy Pickering, and first published in 1917 by Pickering & Inglis (London).

QUOTE: A REMARKABLE TESTIMONY. What but a sterling Christian character and unwearied service out of love of Christ could have produced the following from the world's greatest newspaper *The Times*, which is not given to fulsome flattery:

"Dr Barnardo may be justly ranked among the greatest public benefactors whom England has in recent times numbered among her citizens. With no adventitious aid from fortune or from connections; with no aim but to relieve misery and to prevent sin and suffering, he has raised up a noble monument of philanthropy and of public usefulness."

Proving the Old Book true again: "Them that honour Me I will honour." (I Samuel Chapter 2, verse 30)
UNQUOTE

PART III: TWISTED PATHS

Softly and tenderly, JESUS is calling...
WILL LAMARTINE THOMPSON (1847–1909)

The earliest memory I have of our church is an Easter one. I am about five years old, dressed in a pretty frock, and wearing an Easter bonnet trimmed with flowers.

Accompanied by Matron and all the girls in our cottage, which at that time was Burwell Park, I am being ushered through the lychgate and into the church. There seem to be daffodils everywhere. The stained-glass windows shed their rainbow colours on grown-ups and children alike. The church fills rapidly. The choir moves slowly down the central aisle, singing the processional hymn. The girls are wearing bright blue robes and ugly mortarboard-type hats. The boys look deceptively innocent in their white surplices.

Each cottage had its own 'sitting'. The name was encased in a small brass frame at the beginning of each pew. Leather 'kneelers' hung on hooks in front of the seats. Sitting comfortably on these pews, which had been specially designed for children, must have been a real penance for tall and/or overweight adults! They were also not particularly agreeable for us very small children either. I can recall being prodded for wriggling about when my short legs 'fell asleep'!

All children wore their 'Sunday best'. In summer, I had to wear a horrid ruffledy-puffledy frock, usually covered in polka dots or cissy flowers which *really* offended my tomboy feelings. Regulation Clark's sandals and white ankle socks 'finished me off', but as I grew older I did not have to wear a large bow in my hair.

Sometimes a Panama hat would be worn. Mine always seemed to end up tilting at a rakish angle over one eye. In winter I would shrug myself into a beautifully-cut woollen coat, whilst Matron plonked a large Kangol beret on top of my curls. My legs would be kept snug by long fawn woollen socks. I detested the standard Barnardo winter footwear for girls: stub-toed lace-ups (Clark's again!) which were tan and had to be polished "until you can see your face in them, Susan Plumb!"

The boys were even unluckier fashion-wise. Although some of them were permitted to wear long trousers when they were about fourteen, many of the 'gangly' younger ones must have felt quite resentful in their grey, short-trousered suits. Shirts and ties and black lace-ups completed *their* Sunday best. Their unruly hair would be slicked back with copious applications of hair cream, and their faces presented the unusually scrubbed look seen only on Sundays!

All children were so rigidly monitored that it was almost impossible to misbehave. However, sundry shufflings of feet and bored yawns would be rewarded with either an "I'll deal with you when we get home!" aside, or a hard prod if you were near enough to the matron or master. This depended, of course, on whether the adult had it in for you or was just mildly irritated.

Our church was one of the few places where I could sit quietly and generally be left alone. My favourite window was one that depicted

David with his sling, although it was rather a long way from our pew. I used to wish I could dress like him and be as brave as he must have been to stand up against Goliath of Gath!

At Easter, Harvest Festival and Christmas, our church was always beautifully decorated. 'White' Christmases were especially exciting. We would trudge though the snow, trying not to let it get into our shoes; I don't think we were allowed to wear Wellingtons on Sundays! The bells would be sweetly playing a selection of carols, although the sound might be somewhat muted if there had been a particularly heavy fall of snow.

On Sunday afternoon 'our' matrons used to take some of us to Sunday school outside the Village. Fairlop Gospel Hall was, and still is, situated in Fencepiece Road, opposite what used to be Fairlop Secondary School.

I did not enjoy going to this Sunday school very much though, because I was often the only coloured child there. Sometimes the male teachers attracted my attention and I would gravitate towards them, trying to get them to notice me – my never-ending search for a 'daddy figure'!

There used to be separate classes for children of varying ages, and every year the Sunday school would have an 'Anniversary' celebration. At these I would have some lines from Scripture stories to recite. They would have been drilled into me weeks beforehand.

On the big day, I would stand on the stage in line with other youngsters in my class. When my turn came, I would be prodded to the front of the stage to say my 'piece'. The only recitation I can recall is a strangely apt one!

> *Five stones David took*
> *From the swift-running bed;*
> *And one of them went*
> *In the great giant's head!*

There! Now I'm positive that I've been word perfect!

After the recitations, there would be a huge tea comprising all my favourite goodies: jelly and ice cream, cakes, buns and biscuits! If Matron saw me, she would make me eat sandwiches first. "Bread and butter to start; jelly and cakes after" was the golden rule!

I was very fond of joining in the choruses, but there was one I *loathed*:

> *Jesus loves the little children;*
> *All the children of the world!*
> *Red and yellow, black and white,*
> *All are precious in His sight.*
> *Jesus loves the little children of the world!*

How I dreaded this one! As soon as the word 'black' was reached, several non-Barnardo children would nudge each other and smirk at me. They would nod their heads sagely and mouth, "That's *you!*"

Just inside the door of the hall was a small table. On it was a large metal bust of a black man: 'Our Negro Penny Collector!' He was painted wearing a traditional scarlet jacket, with dazzlingly white collar and cuffs. He had big, 'goggly' eyes. One of his arms had been mechanised so that when a coin was placed in his hand, the arm shot up and tipped the coin into his gaping red mouth. On more than one occasion, I was informed that he was my brother. Oh, those hurtful childish taunts!

To return to the Village; on Sundays, older boys and girls did not have to go to Sunday school but were expected to attend Evensong in our church.

When I became older, I enjoyed this because I was able to sing some of my favourite hymns. The two I liked best were 'The Day Thou Gavest, Lord, Is Ended' and 'Hushed Was the Evening Hymn'. Evensong also became a sort of trysting place for young people, and we girls would 'make eyes' at the boys across the church because, needless to say, girls and boys were carefully segregated.

Sometimes, us girls would be unlucky enough to be sitting in the pew which was directly in front of two formidable Village 'heads', one of whom sung in the choir during Morning Service. These two women were the bane of our young lives! They were expert at intercepting our languishing glances towards the boys' pews. Either one or the other of these ladies would suddenly lean forward and prod the guilty lass painfully between the shoulder blades with a sharp finger. After church, our matrons might be informed of our inattention. Whether or not "deserved" punishment followed depended entirely upon how strict the matron was. I frequently had my pocket money docked of a few pence, or a privilege withheld.

Our Evensong services were fairly 'High Church'. We became familiar with the *Nunc Dimittis* and the *Magnificat*, both of which were sung or, more correctly, rather sweetly intoned, as were all responses. When we came to the 'Glory Be', we would respectfully bow our heads; and, of course, we were all able to recite the Apostles' Creed, heads bowed again at "and in Jesus Christ, His only Son our Lord".

Whenever I entered our church for Evensong, I experienced a curious 'feeling'. Upon mature reflection, I wonder if God was trying to tell me something, even at that young age. If He was, however, I was not ready to listen to Him. I did not like Him very much. Contrary to what I read in Psalm 46, I did *not* find that He was "my refuge; a very present help in trouble". Instead, He was always either not around when I needed Him, or busy making the matrons say such nasty things as "You will never be up to much!" or "You just can't *help* being objectionable: it's in your blood!"

The phrase GOD IS LOVE was drummed into my head at all stages of my spiritual development. But what *was* 'love'? Why was it considered so necessary anyway? The word had no meaning whatever for me, since I had never seen any evidence of it displayed in the Cottage; well, not towards *me* at any rate.

The fault *must* have been mine. Maybe I was one of those girls who were not born to be loved. With a sigh, I would pick up *Uncle Tom's Cabin* and read the part about poor Topsy yet again.

The mistake, of course, was really made by the matrons. I had been brought up to believe implicitly that God put a condition on His love: I must be a good girl – at *all* times. Since I was always being told off or punished for a bewildering array of 'venial sins', it automatically followed that God would not be wasting His precious time on the likes of Susan Plumb!

The unsurprising result of all this negative indoctrination was that I grew to regard any 'presence' of His in my life with both deep suspicion and increasing irritation, which in the long term was to have such a disastrous effect on my 'growth'. I became, in fact, spiritually undernourished.

Until I started to attend Confirmation classes, then, I saw God as being a rather grumpy old man who didn't really like children. At these classes though, I think He might have been trying to steer me tenderly in the right direction. Our vicar at that time was a gentle, loving man, and I grew extremely fond of him. I think he tried hard to help me 'start over', as Americans would say. However, I was now fourteen, and my life in the Cottage was rapidly turning me into an unhappy and moody girl, with very little faith in *anything*, including God. It was a sad case of too little, too late.

The strange thing is that on my Confirmation day, both the matrons gave me presents. Miss C's was a selection of pretty toilet soaps, and Miss D handed me a lovely necklace of bright scarlet glass beads. Whether they themselves bought these gifts for me, or whether they came from Head Office at Stepney, I do not know. However, I still have those beads and one of the boxed soaps – a constant reminder of how much happier my life could have been if the matrons had put some lasting affection into my upbringing.

I sometimes wonder: If I had been allowed to sing in our Village choir, would my life have been different? My reply to this question is always "Yes, I am certain that it would!"

In the film *Amadeus* Salieri says, "All I ever wanted was to sing to God. He *gave* me that longing… If He didn't want me to praise Him with music, why implant the desire, like a lust, in my body and then deny me ...?"

Now, although I would not use the word 'lust' (I prefer to substitute it with the word 'need'), Salieri more than adequately describes how I felt about singing in church.

The desire was planted in me at a very young age, and intensified as I grew.

I can see myself now, eyes shining, standing almost on tiptoe, straight and tense. I am waiting for the introduction to the opening hymn to end. Here it comes! I'm off! My childish treble becomes slightly sharp with the sheer joy of singing. Occasionally I might get a cross glance or a prod and a whispered "Susan Plumb! Stop showing off!" from Matron if I become too exuberant. However, I carry on until the hymn ends. Then I sit down, feeling warm and happy, knowing that from today I will be good and they *will* let me join the choir eventually, because I sing so well! I give a little extra wriggle of joyful anticipation, which elicits yet another repressive glare from Matron.

As I write these words, my eyes cloud over and I give a prolonged sigh, for the non-fulfilment of the dream that could have changed the course of my young life.

It was to be many years before this childhood ambition, to sing in church, was to bear fruit.

In spite of the rather gloomy foregoing, there was to be a silver lining to this spiritual storm cloud; or should I call it 'Balm in Gilead'?

As far back as I can remember, I have had a passion for reading old-fashioned religious literature. I do not know if the books were donated to the Village, or if they were the property of the staff.

All I *do* know is that I revelled in the 'Pansy' books (Hesba Stretton's 'Jessica's First Prayer' was an early favourite) and enjoyed the Religious Tract Society stories, with such titles as '*God's Gift to Two, or Margaret Redfern's Discipline*' and '*Ben Froggatt, or Little Lonesome*'. At the moment of writing, I am immersed in '*Joseph's Little Coat*'.

The books that have had the greatest influence on me, however, are the *Collected Tales of Hy Pickering*, one of which I quoted from in Part II of this chapter.

The fact that I have clung to this type of literature throughout such a turbulent life strengthens my belief that I must, indeed, have been listening out for that Voice all the time!

PART IV: MARY AND ME – COMING HOME

Always we begin again.
ST BENEDICT OF NURSIA (480–547 AD)

Lead, kindly Light, amid the encircling gloom,
Lead Thou me on;
The night is dark, and I am far from home,
Lead Thou me on...
JOHN HENRY, CARDINAL NEWMAN (1801–1900)

INTRODUCTION

In the sleeve notes of this book I have mentioned "A miracle of spiritual and physical healing".

To cut a long, though absorbing, story short, we must travel back to December 2008. I had cracked several ribs when I fell whilst shopping. I was confined to my flat, alone, in pain, and feeling miserable.

Spiritually, I had also been having a tough time, and had reached the stage when I was sure that God had passed me by.

At the end of November, a friend had recommended me to buy "a CD by some men called The Priests. You'll love it: they're Irish!" I would mention here that I had been studying Irish for some months – a beautiful but fiendishly difficult language! I had bought the disc but not yet played it. Now was the time to do so.

As I listened to the disc for the third time, particularly to 'Ave Maria' and 'Be Still My Soul', I began to experience not only an indefinable sense of tranquillity, but a lessening of my physical pain. It is no exaggeration to admit that something was happening to me that was forcing me to confront my problems and reassess my spiritual needs. I began to feel nervous. Where, and how far, would all this lead me?

The months went on. I recovered physically but still felt the necessity to listen to the 'message' contained in this remarkable disc.

However, 'The Priests' were of the Catholic faith and nothing to do with me - or so I thought.

When I realised, then, just over a year ago, that I was being gradually led towards the Catholic faith by The Priests and their 'musical ministry', through God, I was aghast. If *this* happened, it would mean my having to accept MARY, and that simply wasn't possible!

I have already mentioned that our children's church in the Village was rather a 'high' one. However, although I could recite the *Magnificat*, it had no meaning for me at all and was intoned 'parrot fashion'.

Mary never really stood a chance with an emotionally-starved child such as I was. She was always inseparable from her Child. My feelings towards her, from about the age of ten, were probably a combination of envy and resentment. These were, naturally, not expressed in words, but I know that I did not like seeing Jesus being cradled in her arms. No one ever held *me* like that; it wasn't *fair*!

On 'special' Sundays such as Harvest Festival, the girls in our cottage would be taken to an 'outside' church. This was quite a treat, and I can remember walking through cornfields to a church near the old aerodome at Barkingside. Close to the Altar there was a statue of Mary – *and* her Baby, of course. Once again, I was not able to put into words exactly how I felt, but I did think she was looking at me as if she was telling me off!

I measured *all* women by the standards of those who were bringing me up, and clearly the Holy Mother was no exception.

On several occasions, during my time at Fairlop Junior School, I was 'taken to tea' at a teacher's house, but I was never asked to go a second time. Not unnaturally, this made me feel that there was something wrong with me. As a direct result of this, I grew to be an exceptionally prickly child. I felt safer being naughty because then I would not be invited, only to be 'dropped' later on. In short, nothing was going to persuade me to get close to a female: I was too accustomed to being let down by them.

Looking back over the years, however, I now realise that teachers took the children back to their houses for tea by rote. With such huge classes as we had at Fairlop, the chances of *any* child receiving a second invite would of course be extremely remote.

Perhaps the reader can now understand why, *because* of these childhood experiences, my approach towards accepting Mary had been so hesitant.

The most disquieting element I have experienced during the past year has been... an increase in prudishness!

In order to explain how *this* problem raised its troublesome head, I must once again return to my childhood. The reader already knows that I loved singing in church. What he or she is not yet aware of is that, even as a very young child, I questioned words I did not understand – constantly.

It is Christmas time, and I am in our church, attending morning carol service. We have just sung 'A Virgin Most Pure as the Prophets Do Tell'. I am puzzled, but keep quiet until we arrive back at our cottage. Then I ask Matron, "What is a virgin?"

I am given a cross look instead of a direct answer, so I repeat my question. Then Matron purses up her lips and says "Little girls shouldn't ask questions like that!" and I am left with the feeling that the word is a 'rude' one.

This does not satisfy me, so I persist with "If I mustn't know what it means, why do we sing it in church?"

No reply to this, and I am hustled out of the room!

Then there was an even *more* perplexing word contained in the fourth line of verse two of 'Hark! The Herald Angels Sing!' Another puzzle needed to be solved. "Please, Miss, what's a womb?"

That almost brought the dining room round my ears. "It's not a very nice thing to talk about. Get on with your dinner and stop talking so much!"

Of course, over the years, I have had no trouble with these two words. It is only since I started writing my story and thinking deeply about all the aspects of Catholicism that they have troubled me.

The spiritual force that has been leading me towards the Catholic faith has, it is true, enabled me to write about my rather difficult childhood but, oh, it has opened cupboard after cupboard, and from almost every one a grim and dusty skeleton has come rattling out, to unnerve and confuse me.

The most disturbing 'skeleton' I have had to face has been the fact that, although I had no say in the matter at the time, purity and I parted company at a very early stage in my life.

I anticipated problems in saying the Rosary, so of course I found them. If I was going to be a 'good' Catholic, I would *have* to learn how to say it, but, how could I deal with this? Then the idea of adapting the rosary to suit my needs occurred to me:

> *Hail Mary, full of grace;*
> *The Lord is with thee.*
> *Blessed art thou among women and*
> *BLESSED IS THY SON JESUS CHRIST OUR LORD...*
> (Author's capitals)

There! That was much better, and anyway, no one would be listening to me at Mass except God, and He would *certainly* understand!

This problem was not resolved until I went on a 'solo' Retreat early this year. My 'mentor' gently explained to me how important it was for me to realise that Mary's body was indeed "wholly pure" so, regardless of any childhood problems I had gone through, it was all right to say the Rosary correctly. This has been a great comfort to me.

Before I close this section, I have asked myself the question, "Do you have any doubts about being led towards the Catholic faith?"

My reply is "No, but with a proviso." I am not prepared to accept all I hear on the assumption that "if it's in the Missal, it *must* be true". This is far too simplistic.

As a child, I always needed to 'pick to bits' and insist on answers to puzzling words and phrases. As a rather querulous 65-year-old, nothing has changed, except that the need had intensified. I look forward to questioning all aspects of my 'new' faith, and shall expect to receive acceptable answers, or at least have theories put forward that can be discussed in detail!

In Chapter One – Part II, I mentioned how difficult it was for me to try to do a jigsaw puzzle that had no picture on the front of the box.

Amongst the papers handed to me in 1995 was a very old postcard. I did not like it at all; it made me feel uncomfortable and very sad. But I never for a moment considered throwing it away. I now realise why and… here it is!

YES! I have indeed COME HOME.

Virgin and child by David

I was received into the Catholic Church on Wednesday the 2nd of March 2011.

CHAPTER TEN:
From Strength To Strength

Oft in danger, oft in woe

...

Join the war and face the foe;

...

Let not fears your course impede,
Great your strength, if great your need.

HENRY KIRKE WHITE (1785–1806)
F.S. FULLER-MAITLAND (1809–77) & Ors.

PART I: KNOW THYSELF
SOLON (638–558 BC)

I *was* going to commence this final chapter with a message to the people I consider to be the most important among my readers: today's 'troubled teens'.

Upon reflection, however, I have decided that it would make far more sense if I first let them know what I have learnt about *myself* since I left Dr Barnardo's in 1961.

Without, I hope, becoming too long winded, let me state that almost all of my life's experiences have been bought at a very high price. In spite of this, I still feel that I am 'in arrears'. I owe an immense debt of gratitude to Dr Barnardo's, who cared for me during my childhood.

Having read my story, it has no doubt become quite obvious, even to the youngest reader, that Barnardo's made several serious mistakes in the process of bringing me up. I do not hold this against them; not now, anyway.

All parents make mistakes, even in the most loving of what I used to call 'real' families. My Village 'family' was so big that errors of judgement and wrong decisions were bound to occur occasionally. I was only one child, of many, who was to be adversely affected by these.

However, it is only through relating the story of my early life that I have come to believe that I *do* perhaps have something of benefit to pass on to today's young people.

Gloria Steinem once said, "Self-esteem isn't everything; it's just that there's nothing without it!" How true!

Having acknowledged this, I freely admit to several bad points: impatience and occasional intolerance being just two of them. However, a sense of loyalty and a strongly developed social conscience are worth mentioning too, don't you think? although I trust the reader will not consider that I am being pretentious in any way by admitting to these 'assets'.

I will, no doubt, continue to make mistakes in the future, but at least I now feel strong enough to own up to, and profit by them.

I do, indeed, Know Myself…
and my limitations!

PART II: TODAY'S 'TROUBLED TEENS' – A MESSAGE FROM ME TO YOU

Hi! So, you've read my story; *all* of it, I hope! You know that I had quite a tough time as a 'Barnardo kid', but you are also aware that I, in turn, could be feisty and a real pain in the neck sometimes!

Now, without wanting to seem bossy or a know-it-all, here are one or two other facts you need to know… about yourselves!

There's no such thing as turning out bad because you had an awful start in life. OK, so everything's going wrong right now. You feel that the whole world's against you: "I'm too short!", "I'm not as pretty as I'd like to be!", "I feel threatened because I'm black!", "I don't 'fit in' because I'm mixed race!" – the list is endless. Whilst I accept that any of these may be reasons for your feeling undervalued or just plain no good, don't ever make them *excuses* for any sort of rebellious or antisocial behaviour. It simply won't *do!*

You will only end up making enemies in both camps: among your peers, and any adults who might otherwise be prepared to help you.

In Chapter Eight, Part II, I mentioned that there were specially trained people who are more than willing to 'straighten you out' and work *with* you at problem solving. Lucky you!

In *my* day, when I had a problem, I just had to get on with it. No one to listen to me; no one to hold out a helping hand. I might as well have been an 'untouchable' for all they cared!

What's that one of you said? I didn't quite catch it. Oh, you would feel embarrassed, sitting opposite a bloke or a female, telling them how fed up you feel and that everyone has a 'down' on you? Well, you don't *have* to do this! You can do it all on the telephone. "I've got no credit on my mobile!" you moan. So what! Go to the nearest telephone box and dial 0845 90 90 90. That's the Samaritans' number, it's Freephone and open 24/7. By the way, if you are not yet a teenager, *your* number is 0800 11 11. This is Childline. It is also a Freephone number which is open 24/7. Both these organisations will be very understanding and helpful.

To return to the Samaritans, and before we go any further, let me tell you young people out there that I know, from personal experience, just how helpful they are. Yes, I've been there, done that *and* got the postcard! Here's how it all happened.

Over the past fifteen years, I have called the Samaritans on numerous occasions. Once, when I was *very* lonely and unhappy, I actually walked from north-west London to their base near Oxford Street at about four o'clock one bitterly cold morning. The Samaritans were great to me. A cup of hot coffee perked me up and a long one-to-one chat calmed me down.

Take it from one who knows, then; just the fact that these people LISTEN to what you have to say is fantastic. No interruptions; no unwanted advice; no judgmental claptrap. They can also put you in touch with other services that you might need. Go on, try them!

Here's another fact I'm going to throw at you: there's no such thing as having nothing to do these days. No, don't come the "I didn't get any GCSEs so there's no point in trying to get a job" or "I'm BORED, man!' There's nothing interesting to do". The only people, young *or* old, who get bored are... boring people! They mooch around their houses or flats all day. The only 'activities' they seem capable of are opening cans of beer or bottles of juice, lighting up fags or switching on the telly. I've no time for them at all.

You can do better than this! Make a start by getting down to your local Library. It is a mine of information, especially on youth related subjects. You will find that the staff are helpful and more than able to deal with such diverse queries as "When is the next careers Open Day going to be?" or "Where can I go to learn kickboxing?" If they haven't got the info you require in front of them, they will certainly be able to access it on their computer. Off you go!

Ah! One of you has just mumbled that he/she is feeling "too depressed to make any effort to do *anything*!" Well now, the word you used isn't in my personal vocabulary, and never has been. However, if that is how you want to describe yourself, fine! I've got a solution to *that* problem too! How about thinking about someone *else*, for a change?

Ever thought of applying to do voluntary work? There are hundreds of people, less fortunate than yourself, who need help with all sorts of jobs. There are also many organisations who would be grateful for an extra pair of hands to help them deal with their workload. I would just point out, though, that voluntary work in places such as local schools will require that you be police-checked, but once that formality is over, helping out in a school can be very rewarding work (and, yes, I've done that, too, so I'm speaking from experience once again). Who knows? It could lead to your being offered a permanent job, if you are willing to work hard and become a responsible member of the team. Here again, your library can provide details of voluntary organisations in your area.

Still bored? Ever thought about starting a hobby? OK, so stamp collecting, doing jigsaws (I love 'em!), knitting (works wonders for my nerves!), or making model aeroplanes aren't 'cool'. Well, how about basketball or judo? They can become hobbies, too! So can dancing, and there are classes nowadays for every type, from ballroom to breakdance. Music and Movement are wonderful 'stress busters', and you will meet lots of great people.

Once again, I know what I'm talking about! My flat is small, but by changing the sitting room into a bedsit, I have been able to provide myself with a tiny, but serviceable, 'dance studio' in what was once the bedroom. I prance around to every kind of music, from 'Thriller!' to the Charleston, and 'Riverdance'. (I had to save up for a pair of proper tap-shoes for this last-named routine!)

Dancing is fun, it's energetic, and most important of all, it's therapeutic. It makes you happy, *in spite of* yourself. Whether you attend a class or, like me, prefer to hop about the room on your own, is entirely up to you. One last word of advice about it though. Make sure you have a full-length mirror propped up against the wall; it's no fun dancing on your own! One of the best, non-official, therapies around is that of being able to laugh at yourself. Although I am sixty-five, I can still get the giggles when I catch sight of myself in the mirror, especially when I'm doing my Michael Jackson impression!

Life today can be extremely difficult, particularly for teenagers. It can be intimidating; it can leave you feeling isolated and very, very lonely. You get apprehensive about the future and lose confidence in yourself. However, there are people out there who care about you. Life *can* be a lot of fun; but it is up to YOU to be strong and take that first important step forward. No one else can make this decision for you, but believe me, once you've taken that step, you will find it has been well worth the effort. All the best and, God bless!

PART III: FINAL WORDS

I read somewhere that "Children are our heritage. We must cherish them". This might well sound trite. It is, however, very true. With this in mind, I should like to end my story with the following words which are taken from the Holy Bible:

1. At the same time came the disciples unto Jesus, saying, "Who is the greatest in the kingdom of heaven?"
2. And Jesus called a little child unto Him, and set him in the midst of them.
3. And said, "Verily I say unto you, except ye be converted, and become as little children, ye shall not enter into the kingdom of heaven.
4. "Whosoever therefore shall humble himself as this little child, the same is greatest in the kingdom of heaven.
5. "And who so shall receive one such little child in my name receiveth me.
6. "But who so shall offend one of these little ones which believe in me, it were better for him that a millstone were hanged about his neck and that he were drowned in the depth of the sea."

ST MATTHEW Ch. 18 verses 1–6

AMEN